When Jesus told Nicodemus, "You must be born again," He revealed the only way anyone could enter or even see the kingdom of God is as a result of a work of God's Spirit in the heart of a person that is so powerful, so life altering, that it is analogous to physical birth. Just as there is no physical life without physical birth, so there is no spiritual life without spiritual birth. Allen Nelson understands this and helps his readers understand both the nature and importance of this supernatural work of God that takes place inside a person. In the process, Nelson pastorally guides readers over biblical, historical, and theological terrain to help clear up confusion and provide helpful instruction on this vitally important subject. The result is a wonderfully accessible book on a vitally important topic.

—Tom Ascol
Pastor, Grace Baptist Church, Cape Coral, FL, President of Founders Ministries,
President of The Institute of Public Theology

Regeneration is one of the most despised doctrines found within the church. Anyone frequenting "theological" social media will at some point encounter articles, blog posts, and personal comments that spew vile curses at the truth of God sovereignly igniting the dead heart of a sinner and imparting saving faith that transforms the treasonous God-hater into a lover of Christ. Men gnash their teeth at regeneration because it strips them of any participation in their salvation, placing that divine work fully into the hands of God alone. In his book, *A Change of Heart*, pastor Allen Nelson leads a lay-friendly journey into the doctrine of regeneration. He provides key exegetical study, demonstrates the practical outworking of regeneration in the Christian's daily walk with Christ, and shows how this vital doctrine shaped the thinking of believers throughout church history. I hope his hopeful work finds a wide reading among the faithful who desire to think rightly upon this most glorious doctrine.

—Fred Butler
Volunteer Coordinator at John MacArthur's *Grace to You* Media Ministry

If you were to view the empty churches, the vapid worship, and the neutered preaching of the modern American church as the smoldering wreckage of a plane crash, no doubt you would want to find in the rubble the black box in order to find out what went wrong. Looking back in the black box of our church history, you will find one of the central causes of this crash was the abandonment of the doctrine taught in this book. The wings were ripped off. What causes Christianity to soar was removed, and our churches joined the flotsam and jetsam of every other worldview. We need the truth that is found in this book. Allen Nelson elucidates the doctrine of regeneration in these pages with precision and passion. Read this book, believe the truths that are found in it, and, for the love of God and His church, preach the beauties, wonders, and implications of the new birth!

—Wes Brown
Pastor, Plumerville First Baptist Church, Plumerville, AR

Allen Nelson has done it again. Through careful exposition, sound logic, along with the support of great theologians past and present, he has put a spotlight on the doctrine of regeneration. This book will help you understand why so many people claim to be Christians but so very few actually look like Christians. Allen explains how the doctrine of regeneration has been neglected, why this teaching needs to be recovered, and most importantly, how to tell whether you have experienced "a change of heart."

—Harold Smith
Baptist Missionary, Lee Creek Baptist Church, Van Buren, AR

Regeneration is a multi-faceted precious stone that continues to deliver greater and more spectacular beauty the more it is mined. Unequivocally, there exists no sweeter blessing than for the preacher to receive a call or a visit from a person who has attended his services for some time and hear him say, "Pastor, I want to be baptized," and for him to know clearly his way of salvation was given to him by the change wrought of the Holy Spirit in regeneration. Conversely, there is no greater burden the pastor bears than that of the unregenerate church "member."

In *A Change of Heart: Understanding Regeneration and Why It Matters*, Allen has given the church another valuable tool in an effort to assure regenerate church membership. His ability to mine the precious truths from the doctrine of regeneration and present them in a clear and concise manner will be a suitable companion for the churchman who consciously wants to bring glory to God in attending to the church. If you're that churchman, eat this book.

—Tim Rehmer
Pastor/Church Planter, New Jersey

Regeneration is a doctrine that has, in many regards, become a subject of high theology dealt with by professional theologians in journals and seminaries. This is a tragedy because it is a doctrine that is most pertinent in the life of every individual that has lived, lives, or will ever live. It is the doctrine of life eternal. We have seen in our society the effects of placing this doctrine in the "ivory tower." But in *A Change of Heart*, Pastor Allen brings this doctrine back to its rightful place, the local church. From its very dedication: "To the saints of Second Baptist Church of Perryville" (where Allen pastors), the intent of this book is for the church. Pastor Allen walks through the doctrine giving great understanding to the sovereignty of God in it, to man's responsibility, and shows the effects on the life of the believer. It is a great theological treatise from the Scriptures that is flooded with church history and will be both refreshing and insightful to everyone who picks it up. I pray this work finds its way into the hands and eyes of many, and that this will not be the last we hear from this faithful brother.

—Jonathan Murdock
Pastor, Trinity Baptist Church, Port Arthur, TX,
Co-Founder of Fellowship of International Reformed Missions

Not long ago, I was asked to write on the topic, "If Christianity is so good, why are Christians so bad?"—a question made vastly more difficult by the problem of "false professors" in the pews. I'm grateful that Allen Nelson has accessibly, persuasively, and winsomely laid out the case for restricting the title, "Christian," to the regenerate. As *A Change of Heart* negotiates the theological currents and rapids associated with monergism, *Ordo salutis*, sacraments, etc., it's chock-full of Scripture citations, helpful analogies (employing *The Princess Bride*, spinach, buzzards, and a hostage situation), and rich quotes (such as Martyn Lloyd-Jones's "It is true of a man not only that he is in the dark, but that the darkness is also in him") . . . with even a touch of humor (referring to Jesus's John 3 visit to "Nick at Night"). And Nelson's use of other voices is most impressive, so much so that I started grouping them alphabetically to see if every letter was covered. Pretty close, to include this sampling: Augustine and Ascol; Beeke, Berkhof, Bavinck, Bunyan, and Boettner; Calvin, Carson, and Cyprian; Dagg, Edwards, Flavel, Grudem, Hodge, Judson, Keach, Luther, MacArthur, Nettles, Owen, Packer, Reisinger, Sproul, Tertullian, Vaughan, and, for W, Wesley, Whitefield, Watson, and Washer.

When I was a trustee at Southern [Baptist Theological Seminary] back in the 1980s, a candidate for tenure was working at cross-purposes with the Abstract of Principles' Article VI on "The Fall of Man," which states that Adam's "posterity inherit a nature corrupt and wholly opposed to God and His law." I wish that she'd had this book on hand to help clear up her thinking.

–Dr. Mark Coppenger
Retired Professor of Christian Philosophy and Ethics, Southern
Baptist Theological Seminary

A CHANGE OF HEART

A CHANGE OF HEART

UNDERSTANDING REGENERATION
AND WHY IT MATTERS

ALLEN S. NELSON IV

A Change of Heart: Understanding Regeneration and Why It Matters

Copyright © 2023 by Allen S. Nelson IV

All rights reserved. No part of this book may be used or reproduced in any manner whatsoever without written premission except in the case of brief quotations embodied in critical articles and reviews.

Published by:

Free Grace Press
815 Exchange Ave., Ste. 101
Conway, AR 72032

Email: support@freegracepress.com
Website: freegracepress.com

Printed in the United States of America

Scripture quotations, unless otherwise indicated, are from the ESV® Bible (The Holy Bible, English Standard Version®), copyright © 2001 by Crossway, a publishing ministry of Good News Publishers, Used by Permission. All rights reserved.

Cover design by Scott Schaller

ISBN: 978-1-7338517-1-8

For additional Reformed Baptist titles, please visit our website at freegracepress.com

Dedicated to
The saints of Perryville Second Baptist Church.
It is one of the greatest joys of my life to be your pastor.
Thank you for your love for Christ and His doctrine,
and for your eagerness to grow in the Lord.

"To be saved by grace supposeth that God hath taken the salvation of our souls into his own hand; and to be sure it is safer in God's hand than ours."

- *John Bunyan (1628-1688)*

CONTENTS

Part I: Introducing Regeneration . . . 15

1. The Heart of the Matter . . . 17
2. Mere Christianity . . . 27
3. Family History . . . 41

Part II: What It Means to Be Regenerated (Born Again) . . . 55

4. You *Must* Be Born Again: The Necessity of Regeneration (Part I) . . . 57
5. The Natural Man: The Necessity of Regeneration (Part II) . . . 71
6. Mongerism: God's Sovereignty in Regeneration . . . 81
7. Really New: The Totality of Regeneration . . . 97
8. Lasting Change: The Longevity of Regeneration . . . 111

Part III: Why Regeneration Matters . . . 121

9. Because the Bible Is Trustworthy . . . 123
10. Because the Holy Spirit Is God . . . 135
11. Because the Local Church Is for Believers . . . 147
12. Because the Ordinances Are Beautiful . . . 163
13. Because Authentic Evangelism Is Essential . . . 179

Appendix: John Flavel on the Glory of God's Work in Regeneration . . . 199

PART I

INTRODUCING REGENERATION

1
THE HEART OF THE MATTER

The electrocardiogram graph glowed an iridescent green against the black backdrop of the monitor. A constant high-pitched droning sound accompanied the flat line readout. The nodules might as well have been connected to a lump of clay. There was no heartbeat to be found.

The motionless young man enjoyed unrivaled fitness. Though his body was decades younger than it appeared to be, this was not a sign of poor health. So much potential lay before him. The Physician, more aware of the man's condition than any other, continued the momentous task at hand. "Physician" does not quite capture the fullness of the situation. Artist? Perhaps. Then again, it's unfair to assign to only one common noun the responsibility to bear the weight of the moment.

A surgical procedure would begin later in the day, but that was not the skill required at this instant. Rest would be tomorrow. Today, the labor persisted. A sense of love, care, and creative genius permeated every movement.

The extraordinary procedure continued while a host of bewildered eyes fixated upon the display of expertise. It was all so similar to things they had seen done before and yet, also very new.

Truth be told, it was the first time such a feat had ever been performed. Still, everything was going according to plan. Beyond a shadow of a doubt, there were no better hands for the lifeless man to be in. This day, a Friday of all days, carried such promise that it would forever leave a mark upon not just the man but all of humanity itself.

Then in a moment everything changed. The monotone sound coming from the monitor became a repetitive beep. Electrical activity from the chest could be detected. The flat line changed into waves. The man's toes wiggled. His eyes opened. His brain began to think. His lungs filled with oxygen. *Life*.

Adam, of course, was not really connected to a heart monitor. God needed no such machine to display His majesty before the watching creation. Instead, Yahweh demonstrated His glory through His special involvement on the sixth day "forming" man out of the dust of the earth.[1] Then, the Lord God stooped to the man and breathed into his nostrils, causing him to become a living being.

We are fearfully and wonderfully made indeed! Life began with the sovereign initiative of the Almighty. He asked no one's permission. He needed no one's assistance. He just did it out of His love, wisdom, and power. All for His glory.[2]

Had there been a monitor, its readings would be off the charts. Blood pumped vigorously through Adam's veins. The first man was now in possession of one of the most fascinating organs in the human body, a beating heart.

---

[1] R. C. Sproul, ed., *The Reformation Study Bible: English Standard Version* (Orlando: Reformation Trust, 2015), 14.

[2] I've taken some liberty in telling the creation of Adam but have sought to remain faithful to the Scriptures.

THE GLORY OF THE HUMAN HEART

The average person gets somewhere around three billion ticks. When you set this book down and wait until tomorrow to pick it back up again, you will have gone through another 100,000 of them. That's quite a workload for the fist-sized, 9 to 12-ounce little ticker located in the middle of your chest known as the heart– "a hollow muscular organ of vertebrate animals that by its rhythmic contraction acts as a force pump maintaining the circulation of the blood."[3]

The same vascular organ that began beating inside Adam's chest thumps inside of you at this moment, creating every day "enough energy to drive a truck 20 miles. In a lifetime, that is equivalent to driving to the moon and back."[4] What marvelous work God did in fashioning an organ as wonderful as the human heart!

Of course, you did not pick this book up to learn interesting facts about the cardiovascular system. Good thing. This is a theology book. The heart we are examining is a bit more complicated than your physical blood pumper.

THE HEART OF MAN

If we aren't talking about the cardiovascular system in this book, what, then, is this heart I speak of? The Tinman told Dorothy that he wanted a heart "to register emotion, jealousy, devotion..." Is this the heart then? Just the opposite of the head? One thinks in the brain, but *feels* in the heart? Unsurprisingly, Hollywood doesn't give us an accurate depiction of the heart.

The biblical understanding of the heart is not merely sentimental or emotional. In Matthew 9:4, for example, Jesus asked the scribes, "Why do you *think* evil in your hearts?" (emphasis mine). Thus, the heart not only feels but thinks! That's not all. The *Dictionary of Biblical Languages* gives one definition of the Hebrew word for "heart" as,

---

[3] *Merriam-Webster's Collegiate Dictionary* (Springfield, MA: Merriam-Webster, 2003), s.v. "heart."

[4] This quote and the above information on the human heart are taken from https://www.sunwaymedical.com.

"the source of life of the inner person in various aspects, with a focus on feelings, thoughts, volition, and other areas of the inner life."[5] Here we learn that the heart of man is essentially the totality of his inner life.

Puritan John Owen (1616-1683) notes, "The heart in the Scripture is variously used; sometimes for the mind and understanding, sometimes for the will, sometimes for the affections, sometimes for the conscience, sometimes for the whole soul."[6] Never accused of being a man of few words, Owen goes on to write how the heart inquires, discerns, judges, chooses, refuses, avoids, warns, and determines.[7]

Thus, the life Adam received in the garden was more than mere animal life. God did not create Adam as a Tinman. Not only did the breath of life cause Adam's heart to beat, it also made him a living soul, having a conscience, affections, desire, and a will, all of which we refer to as his "heart." God gave Adam a physical heart, while also giving him a *heart*.

When we speak of the human heart in this way, we are talking about the very core of who we are. Every time the Bible speaks of the heart it is referencing, at least in part, the entirety of the inner man. The heart of man is that non-material part of each person that makes us who we really are. From it comes our desires, thoughts, will, motives, etc.

The Creator of the heart teaches us in His Book that the heart thinks, feels, and acts. Is there a better One to tell us about this heart than God Himself? The Bible shows us, then, that the heart is both who we are and the determining factor for what we do. We do what we do *because of* who we are. This is true of all men, women, boys, and girls.

---

[5] James Swanson, *Dictionary of Biblical Languages with Semantic Domains: Hebrew* (Oak Harbor, WA: Logos Research Systems, 1997).
[6] John Owen, *The Works of John Owen*, ed. William H. Goold, Vol. 6 (Edinburgh: T&T Clark), 170.
[7] Owen, *The Works of John Owen*, Vol. 6, 170.

Thus, we cannot separate our heart from who we are. The person does a foul deed but then inaccurately states, "Oh but my heart was in the right place." Wrong. What we do flows out of the heart because it is who we are. God created Adam as a living being and we do not pretend that our outward material self is somehow separated from our inward immaterial self. This is a package deal. Body and soul go together, making us the people that we are.

THE DARK SIDE OF THE HEART

The heart we are examining, then, is a bit funny. Its perplexity confounds the mind. I mean, no one—no mere mortal that is—has ever even seen it. This heart cannot be studied in a lab or weighed upon a scale. At the same time, however, this heart can be broken or cause us pain or bring us happiness. All of this intrigues us toward its mystery.

But this heart is far more than just perplexing and mysterious. Left to itself, it's also sinister. Philip Graham Ryken writes, "The human heart cannot be trusted, cannot be healed, cannot be understood. It is devious, incurable, and inscrutable."[8] Or, commenting on Jeremiah 17:9, John Gill writes, "The heart is deceitful to a very great degree, it is superlatively so."[9]

Really, then, the human heart is a convolution of corruption—an intricacy of iniquity. On the one hand, it possesses enough of the image of God that it truly desires to love and be loved. On the other hand, it is in such a state of sin and misery that what it consistently desires is actually most detrimental to our very existence.

This is the dark side of the heart. We are not in Eden anymore. Though all mankind today shares in the physical life of Adam, we have also inherited what he obtained for us in Genesis 3, death.

---

[8] Philip Graham Ryken, *Jeremiah and Lamentations: From Sorrow to Hope*, Preaching the Word (Wheaton: Crossway, 2001), 279.
[9] John Gill, *An Exposition of the Old Testament*, Vol. 5, Baptist Commentary Series (London: Mathews and Leigh, 1810), 498.

This not only means that we will all physically die, but also that we begin life now as those who are dead spiritually. We enter this world now with the need for a change of heart.

HEART WORSHIP

God created our first parents to glorify and enjoy Him forever. Satan deceived Eve as to her purpose, and Adam outright rejected God's goodness toward him by disobeying His command. This couple sought to be like God and ultimately directed their worship unto themselves instead of their Creator. The human heart now seeks to glorify *self* and enjoy it forever.

Jesus said, "[O]ut of the heart come evil thoughts, murder, adultery, sexual immorality, theft, false witness, [and] slander" (Matt. 15:19). The human heart after Eden is in such a state of corruption that it yearns for the wrong things. *It finds itself in a perpetual state of dissatisfaction because it cannot ever fully achieve that for which it fervently aches, namely the glory of self.* The heart – sometimes secretly, and sometimes rather openly – constantly pushes self-promotion, self-preservation, self-entitlement, self-ad nauseum.

If only the whole world, God Himself, and the host of heaven above would bow down and worship *self,* then the heart might be satisfied. But even that would not suffice! The Lord designed the heart only to worship the Infinite. Even the self-glory the heart seeks will not lastingly gratify.

Are you beginning to get a better picture of the bedlam that lies at the core of human existence? See, when someone says, "just follow your heart," what they are *really* communicating is "just do what will most please yourself." This is terrible advice. Abhorrent really.

Left to itself, the human heart is dastardly deceitful and desperately disordered (cf. Jer. 17:9). It may or may not acknowledge its Maker, but its chief desire is to exalt itself above all else. If it could force others to worship it, it would do it – in a heartbeat. Certain despots throughout history have proven as such.

As the old preacher once said, "What's down in the well comes out in the bucket." We see this in our culture daily. People's lives are consistently ordered around their heart's object of affection. Since the heart's treasure is self, we constantly see sins like greed, lust, lies, and murder before our eyes. We even see, in the name of self-exaltation, the self-mutilation of bodies as people reject their God-given gender in order to assume a faux reality. Their love of self is causing them to destroy themselves. "Claiming to be wise they became fools..." (Rom. 1:22).

Jesus said, "For where your treasure is, there your heart will be also" (Matt. 6:21). The road-rager, porn addict, transgender woman, workaholic absentee father, and single mom living vicariously through her daughter all have one thing in common: They are treasuring, i.e., worshiping, self.

THE HEART OF CHRISTIANITY

The human heart, along with its treasure, is foundational to understanding Christianity. At its core, Christianity centers on the gospel of Jesus Christ, the Son of God, and His full equality with the Father and Holy Spirit, His incarnation, obedience, fulfilling all righteousness, propitiatory substitution, death, burial, resurrection, exaltation, and return. The only proper response to this message is for one to forsake all else and believe on Christ alone as his or her only suitable and all-sufficient Savior.

Those who have responded in this way to this message cherish Christ. Fundamentally, this is what constitutes a Christian – one whose heart has turned away from self and toward Christ. He or she is one who now desires to glorify God and enjoy Him forever.

Sadly, many today, some who even profess to follow Jesus, cannot accurately define what a Christian is. At the heart of the definition is treasure. To be a Christian is to treasure Christ supremely (cf. Matt. 13:44). Those who do not treasure Christ supremely, treasure self ultimately. Look around our culture today – both the culture at large and the evangelical culture – and you can see, it's not Christ who captivates our hearts.

A person lives, thinks, and acts differently when Christ is the heart's treasure. Those who treasure Jesus deny self and follow Him, having hope beyond this life only (cf. 1 Cor.15:19). The Christian's ultimate longing is more for that Celestial City that is to come than for the successes and accolades of this passing world (cf. Heb. 11:10).

In sum, to be a Christian is to have had *a change of heart* – a heart that moves from adoring self to treasuring Christ. As Jonathan Edwards wrote, "To follow Christ in heart, is to have a heart to follow him."[10] A Christian is someone with a change of heart – a heart that has been made new by a work of sovereign grace. This is the doctrine of "regeneration" or being "born again."[11]

A true Christian is one who has undergone a transformation of heart. No one can change their immaterial heart any more than they can change out their physical heart. God is the changer of hearts for His own glory.

A doctor tells a man he is overweight and needs to change or he will die. And let's say the doctor gives the man a plan to eat and exercise well. We will call it the ABC's of losing weight. Let's say the man goes through the steps properly. He begins eating and exercising well and loses a hundred pounds.

To whom does glory belong? The doctor? Or the man? Well, the man couldn't have done it without the doctor, but the man is the one who finally accomplished it. Praise the Lord for good doctors! But it was the man who did the work. The quarterback threw a terrific pass, but the receiver still had to make the effort to catch the ball. Good teamwork.

What about a different man who is on the operating table and dies. Can this man resuscitate himself? Of course not! But thankfully, he has a doctor who works and works and works and ends up reviving the man. Because of this, the man makes it out and reunites with his family.

---

[10] Thomas S. Kidd, *America's Religious History: Faith, Politics, and the Shaping of a Nation* (Grand Rapids: Zondervan Academic, 2019), 37.
[11] We will give a formal definition of regeneration in Chapter 2.

Who do you give the glory to then? The man who was dead on the table? What did he do? *Nothing*. You give all the glory to the doctor for his work because he did it all. No teamwork here. This is the golfer sinking a hole in one.

So too, in regeneration, we give God alone all the glory for His sovereign work. God does not give us the ABCs of salvation and then reward us with a new heart for following His steps. He works for us, not with us. We could do nothing to bring about our new birth. God did it all!

Thomas Manton wrote, "Men cannot drive out self-love. It must be another more powerful love, which must draw them from love of self; as one nail drives out another."[12] God alone is the One who drives out our self-love with love for Himself by replacing our old heart with a new one.

Christians, therefore, bow their heads in humble adoration saying, in the words of Jeff Johnson, "It was God who intervened and quickened us from our spiritual deadness. By grace—and by grace alone—we have been born again."[13] Creation looked on as God breathed life into the first man. Just as that divine action caused the blood to flow through Adam's veins, so too does God breathe spiritual life into the hearts of His people causing them to place their faith in Him and repent from sin. And now the angels rejoice (Luke 15:7).

But before pushing too far ahead, we need to back up and get a wider picture of our current evangelical predicament. We need to take evangelicalism to the doctor's office for a check-up. Prepare yourself. The results will not be for the faint of heart.

---

[12] Charles Spurgeon, *Flowers from a Puritan's Garden: Spurgeon on the Statements of Truth from the Writings of Thomas Wanton* (Lexington, KY: CreateSpace Independent Publishing Platform, 2017, 1883 original), 119.
[13] Jeffrey D. Johnson, *The Sovereignty of God* (Conway, AR: Free Grace, 2023), 157.

2
MERE CHRISTIANITY

Heading to the doctor's office as an adult is the complete opposite of when you were a child. When you were a child, you went to the doctor, were told how good you were, maybe got a little game or sticker from the nurse, and then your mom or grandmother took you out for ice cream afterward. When you go to the doctor as an adult, you are told how much better you need to be while being told you need to eat less ice cream and play fewer games, so you can be more active!

Going for a regular check-up may not be fun anymore, but it's a necessary aspect of healthy living. This is particularly true when something is off. When something seems to not be working properly, we need someone to diagnose the issue so that we can get the help we need. This holds true spiritually too. Something is off in evangelicalism today. We are long overdue for a check-up.

Historically, an evangelical is someone who sees the Bible as his or her highest authority and understands the need for every person to have a personal experience of conversion in embracing the gospel of Jesus Christ in repentance and faith. Truth be told, the evangelical movement has come apart at the seams in the last few decades - so much so that the word "evangelical" is becoming increasingly nebulous, almost rendering it altogether meaningless. There are several underlying causes for this unraveling, but the hypothetical "evangelical check-up" would reveal one crucial diagnosis: we have lost the Scriptural understanding of what it means to be a Christian.

We have reached a crisis point where many self-identifying evangelicals cannot even give a biblical definition of a Christian. They typically classify a Christian as someone who can affirm the lowest common denominator of mere Christianity. They profess Jesus but don't dig too much under the surface of who or what that profession entails.[14] The idea of church is a good idea, but "being the church" is now more important than "going to church."[15] They believe in heaven, but eternal judgment is now negotiable.[16]

As Jim Domm aptly states, "How many there are who rest satisfied with a mere nominal Christianity. Many are content with a form of godliness that has no power (2 Tim. 3:5)."[17] Too many evangelicals today do not understand biblical Christianity.

At the heart of Christianity, *literally, the heart*, is the doctrine we are addressing in this book – the powerful work of the Holy Spirit in the new birth, i.e., the doctrine of regeneration. Regeneration is simply the theological term for being born again. It is spiritual *life*. For a person to have a heart that treasures Christ and not self, he or she must be born again.

---

[14] 43% of evangelicals surveyed in *The State of Theology* survey said Jesus was not God. Statement 7 (2022), https://thestateoftheology.com.

[15] It is impossible to "be the church" without gathering regularly with the church. A recent example of the disconnect between Christianity and the local church is shown in the 2022 *The State of Theology survey*. 54% of evangelicals agreed that "Worshiping alone or with one's family is a valid replacement for regularly attending church." Statement 22, thestateoftheology.com.

[16] It is actually even worse than this. In *The State of Theology* survey of 2022, 56% of evangelicals polled agreed that "God accepts the worship of all religions, including Christianity, Judaism, and Islam." Over half of professing evangelicals are saying Christianity doesn't even matter since God accepts the worship of all! Statement 3, thestateoftheology.com.

[17] Rob Ventura, General Editor, *A New Exposition of The London Baptist Confession of Faith of 1689* (Fearn, Scotland: Christian Focus, 2022), 191.

Early evangelicals understood that regeneration "is the very hinge on which the salvation of each of us turns."[18] In the 21st centruy, however, many seem to not understand this precious doctrine. They are not the first. Not everyone understood this during Jesus's day either.

NICODEMUS

One night in 1st century Jerusalem, a man of the Pharisees went in for an unplanned spiritual checkup. The Great Physician Himself gave Nicodemus a diagnosis that left him as puzzled as many evangelicals seem to be today.

Consider the narrative from John 3:1-2. "Now there was a man of the Pharisees named Nicodemus, a ruler of the Jews. This man came to Jesus by night and said to him, 'Rabbi, we know that you are a teacher come from God, for no one can do these signs that you do unless God is with him.'"

Nicodemus was a member of the Sanhedrin. The Sanhedrin was the last stop on matters of Jewish law and religion before the Romans got involved. So, Nicodemus was not your average Jew. He "was not merely a man—he was quite a man."[19]

Some commentators suspect what Nicodemus was doing here was trying to understand who Jesus is. It was in the Sanhedrin's best interest to know who was teaching what and to keep some form of authority over the teaching that took place. In a sense, that's not necessarily a bad thing. It's a good thing to want proper teachers teaching proper doctrine. But in another sense, of course, we end up seeing that in the New Testament this desire played itself out practically as a matter of control rather than serious concern for God's Word.

Nicodemus, at least outwardly, seems to think favorably of this Rabbi and His work. After all, he affirms that God sent Him. Nicodemus has taken notice of this Teacher, and something about

---

[18] George Whitefield, *Selected Sermons of George Whitefield* (Oak Harbor, WA: Logos Research Systems, Inc., 1999), Sermon 49.
[19] Richard D. Phillips, *Jesus the Evangelist: Learning to Share the Gospel from the Book of John* (Lake Mary, FL: Reformation Trust, 2007), 59–60.

Him has warranted a night-time approach. Why does he come after sunset? We do not know this for sure. It could be that he did not want the rest of the Sanhedrin to know. Or it could be that this was an appropriate time to question Jesus after a busy day. Regardless of his motivations, here he is at night. Here he is, flattering Jesus.

THE CONFRONTATION

Jesus, though, looks past Nicodemus's outward civility. He dismisses small talk and gets to the point. These words, like a sharp two-edged sword, cut right to the heart of the matter and, not coincidentally, to Nicodemus's heart as well.

"Truly, truly, I say to you, unless one is born again he cannot see the kingdom of God" (John 3:3). Jesus pushes through the fluff and steers the conversation directly to the root issue. This is a masterful tactic of our Lord – moving immediately to the foundational concerns at hand. But He often does so in a way that can be initially confusing, raising more questions.

Jesus's response catches Nicodemus so off guard that he asks, "How can a man be born when he is old? Can he enter a second time into his mother's womb and be born?" And here we find one objective of this book – to answer Nicodemus's first question. We want to consider how it is that a man can be born when he is old and what exactly Jesus means when He says, "Truly, truly, I say to you, unless one is born again he cannot see the kingdom of God."

The word "truly" is the Greek word for "amen." Jesus speaks this way 25 times in the gospel of John. He does so to draw special attention to the veracity of His teaching. He Himself is the Amen (Rev. 3:14) and truth (John 14:6). His words are life (John 6:63b), and anyone who keeps His word will never see death (John 8:51). Truly, truly, then, it behooves us to take an entire book to consider what Jesus believes it means to be born again.

REGENERATION

John 3 is not the first time we see birthing language in the gospel of John. John 1:12-13 states, "But to all who did receive him, who believed in his name, he gave the right to become children of God, who were born, not of blood nor of the will of the flesh nor of the will of man, but of God."

John 3:7 will not be the last time we see this concept either. In John 6:63a, Jesus says, "It is the Spirit who gives *life;* the flesh is no help at all." So, the idea of the new birth and new life are repeated themes from Jesus in the Gospel of John. In every instance it is revealed to be a work of God and not initiated, produced, or aided by the idea, will, or flesh of man. Just as Adam lay lifeless in the Garden until God breathed upon him, so too do the spiritually dead remain in that state until the Spirit of God shines forth in their hearts (cf. 2 Cor. 4:6).

This brings us back to the theological term – *regeneration*. At its base, regeneration is about a change of heart, but I want to give you a few more formal definitions. We will start with the Southern Baptist Convention's (the largest evangelical denomination in the United States) statement of faith, the Baptist Faith and Message (2000).

It reads, "Regeneration, or the new birth, is a work of God's grace whereby believers become new creatures in Christ Jesus. It is a change of heart wrought by the Holy Spirit through conviction of sin, to which the sinner responds in repentance toward God and faith in the Lord Jesus Christ."[20]

We see here that regeneration is a work of God's grace. That's what Jesus says in John 3 (and John 1 and John 6) – being born again is a work of the Holy Spirit. It's not about genes, jumping through hoops, or ingenuity, but *sovereign grace.*

Another definition comes from theologian Wayne Grudem. He defines regeneration as, "A secret act of God in which he imparts new spiritual life to us; sometimes called 'being born again.'"[21] Jesus

---

[20] It also adds, "Repentance and faith are inseparable experiences of grace."
[21] Wayne Grudem, *Systematic Theology: An Introduction to Biblical Doctrine* (Grand Rapids: Zondervan, 1994), 1253.

says in John 3:8, "The wind blows where it wishes, and you hear its sound, but you do not know where it comes from or where it goes. So it is with everyone who is born of the Spirit."

Regeneration, then, is both supernatural (since it is a work of the Spirit of God) and "a secret act" – you don't see it happen; you only see the effects of it. Regeneration is the most miraculous, glorious work that God performs in the soul of man. To misunderstand or diminish this crucial doctrine of being born again is to slight the glory of God!

Finally, the late J.I. Packer (1926-2020) defines regeneration this way, "Regeneration is the spiritual change wrought in the heart of man by the Holy Spirit in which his/her inherently sinful nature is changed so that he/she can respond to God in Faith, and live in accordance with His Will."[22]

We've seen some important words repeated in these definitions. We've seen the words "new" and "spiritual." We've also seen that each description has at least hinted at the idea of a total transformative change. The Christian message is not about sick people in need of medicine. It's not merely that people are immoral and simply need to amend their ways to do better. It's not that people need to learn new stuff or enact more laws. It's not even ultimately that people are oppressed and need justice. It's not about modifying behavior.

No, the Christian message is, you must be born again. Regeneration is *a change of heart*.

A Christian is a person who has a new heart (cf. 2 Cor. 5:17). We will talk about why a new heart is needed in a future chapter, but for now we need to understand that regeneration is a total overhaul. And it is God the Holy Spirit, through the resurrection of Christ, who brings about this change of heart we stand so desperately in need of.

---

[22] https://www.monergism.com/thethreshold/articles/onsite/packer_regen.html. Packer goes on to say, "It extends to the whole nature of man, altering his governing disposition, illuminating his mind, freeing his will, and renewing his nature."

AN ACT OF GOD

The Scriptures are clear that God is not only the Creator of the human heart but also its *recreator*. God breathed life into Adam. Adam, in return, plunged mankind into sin and misery. Therefore, neither Adam nor his offspring can get back what was lost in the Garden.

The human heart began with a sovereign act of God, and in order for mankind to have a change of heart, it too must be of the sovereign will and work of the Almighty. As one early church father noted, commenting on Psalm 85:6, "[O]ur being made alive is from Thee."[23] Just as Adam could never have breathed life into himself as he laid inanimately in the Garden, neither can a spiritually dead man or woman breathe spiritual life into themselves.

A change of heart, then, is all of God, in God, by God, through God, and for God's glory. This is possible because of the gospel – through the resurrection of Jesus Christ from the dead (cf. 1 Peter 1:3).

Stephen Charnock wrote, "it is good to be sensible of our own impotency, that God may have the glory of His own grace."[24] When we minimize what we will address in Part II of this book, namely, the necessity, sovereignty, totality, and longevity of regeneration, we slight God's glorious work in salvation and end up exalting man.

Regeneration must be an act of God alone. Insurance companies today continue to talk about "acts of God." The Hartford Insurance company notes, "Disastrous events can happen when you least expect them. When they're outside of human control, they're described as an Act of God. The phrase Act of God refers to an accident or other natural event caused *without human intervention* that could not have been prevented by reasonable foresight or care."[25]

---

[23] Augustine of Hippo, "Expositions on the Book of Psalms," in *Saint Augustin: Expositions on the Book of Psalms*, ed. Philip Schaff, trans. A. Cleveland Coxe, Vol. 8, A Select Library of the Nicene and Post-Nicene Fathers of the Christian Church, First Series (New York: Christian Literature Company, 1888), 406.

[24] Stephen Charnock, *A Discourse of the Efficient of Regeneration*, Part I. Accessed: https://www.sacred-texts.com/chr/charnock/cha05.htm.

[25] https://www.thehartford.com/aarp/homeowners-insurance/act-of-god (emphasis mine).

It is interesting to me how every so often insurance companies can be so theological. They recognize an act of God as something caused apart from human intervention. Further, these events are called "acts of God" because no one can doubt they happened. If you have ever seen a town hit by a tornado you do not wonder if something really happened there or not. It's too obvious.

If only more evangelicals were so theological when it comes to understanding the changing of the human heart as an act of God. Regeneration is outside human control. It is an act that is undeniable. As the hurricane leaves its undeniable mark on the coastal city, so the hand of God leaves its mark on the soul that has been brought from death to life.

This is why Part III of this book is devoted to the functional outworking of regeneration: God's initial act of changing the heart cannot be seen but its effects most certainly can be, and a proper understanding of the doctrine of regeneration matters greatly. We must not only understand why and how a change of heart comes about, but also take into account the practical ramifications this understanding has on our everyday life. To go wrong in our understanding of the doctrine of regeneration is like driving a car with bad tires. Initially, we may feel like we are getting around alright, but eventually it is going to cause us some trouble down the road.

THE ORDO SALUTIS

Let me map out now where I find regeneration within the *Ordo Salutis* – this is the Latin phrase meaning "order of salvation." What we are trying to think through here is where in the "process" of salvation a person's change of heart occurs. After mapping this out, we will take all the data we've digested in these first two chapters and seek to give a more formal definition of what constitutes a Christian.

Note that I am mainly dealing with the *Ordo Salutis* "in time." If I were going outside of time, I would begin with unconditional election, but I leave that out purposefully to demonstrate that the first two items on my list below can and do happen at times to unbelievers. But once the effectual drawing of the Holy Spirit happens, a person is moved from death to life, resulting in their conversion to Christianity.

First, on my list in time, then, I put gospel proclamation. God designed *gospel proclamation* to go out to all persons. Every person who hears the gospel responds to it—one way or another. Sadly, many hear the gospel and respond by choosing to reject it. Some hear it and respond with acceptance, by God's grace. Any person who becomes a Christian must first have heard the gospel. Faith comes by hearing and hearing by the word of Christ (Rom. 10:17).

Next comes *conviction of sin*. Consider this vivid and helpful explanation from Dr. Curt Daniel,

> Just as a physical birth has birth pains, so does the spiritual birth. It is called conviction of sin (John 16:8). The Holy Spirit does this as He prepares us for the new birth. He takes the holy law of God and burns it into our consciences in a deeper way than ever before. We do more than feel guilty; we know we are lost and doomed. The Puritans used to call this law-work (not to be confused with a work of the law). It is painful and devastating. We resist it, and the more we fight it the worse it becomes. It is painful to kick against God's work (Acts 26:14). God thus breaks open the soil to plant the seed. Conviction is the needle of the law piercing us in order to pull the thread of salvation. No conviction, no conversion. But God turns the pain to joy in due time.[26]

No one becomes a Christian without first understanding their need for Christ. Yet, some people do feel conviction for sin without being converted. It is during this conviction of sin that one of two things happens. Either the sinner becomes "alarmed," like Felix (Acts 24:24-27), and seeks a way out of the conviction. That may happen from doubling down on sin or even becoming antagonistic toward Christianity.

---

[26] Curt Daniel, *Basic Christian Doctrines* (Conway, AR: Free Grace, 2021), 188.

The sinner may also try to get out of the conviction of sin by religious reform. Instead of running to Christ he or she runs to outward duty and goes through the motions of Christianity, even for decades, in order to suppress guilt. 17th-century English independent pastor, Matthew Mead, noted, "The ground of many a man's engaging in religion is the trouble of his conscience".[27]

The point is, the sinner becomes convicted, but instead of yielding to Christ only hardens his or her own heart against Him. So, some persons remain unregenerate in spite of the fact that they have both heard the gospel and been convicted of their sin. They have chosen to strengthen their resistance instead of surrendering to King Jesus.

The other thing that might happen through conviction of sin is that the Holy Spirit may continue to graciously move in such a way as to confront the sting of the Law with the healing balm of the gospel and effectually draw the sinner to Christ. "Effectual" simply means "producing...a desired effect."[28] Thus, when a sinner is *effectually* called by God, the Holy Spirit commences His sovereign overcoming of the sinner's hostilities and initiates the divine procedure of heart surgery.

The result is the Holy Spirit miraculously raising the sinner from spiritual death to spiritual life, (cf. Eph. 2:5) having given the sinner a new heart. That new believer joyfully responds in repentance toward God and faith in the Lord Jesus, and is thus justified by grace alone through faith alone and adopted as a son or daughter of the Most High and Holy God.

It is essential to understand the intimate connection between the effectual call and regeneration. The Second London Baptist Confession of 1689 states,

> Those whom God hath predestinated unto life, he is pleased in his appointed, and accepted time, effectually to call, by his Word and Spirit, out of that state of sin and

---

[27] Matthew Mead, *The Almost Christian Discovered* (1661). Accessed: https://gracegems.org/28/matthew_mead3.htm.
[28] *Merriam-Webster's Collegiate Dictionary*, 2003.

death in which they are by nature, to grace and salvation by Jesus Christ; enlightening their minds spiritually and savingly to understand the things of God; taking away their heart of stone, and giving unto them a heart of flesh; renewing their wills, and by his almighty power determining them to that which is good, and effectually drawing them to Jesus Christ; yet so as they come most freely, being made willing by his grace."[29]

In one sense, regeneration originates in the effectual call, and its result is faith in Christ and repentance from sin. As Sinclair Ferguson writes, "There is no regeneration which is not expressed in both faith and repentance."[30] Because of regeneration, the Christian chooses to place his or her faith in Christ and is justified before God on the merits of Christ alone, adopted as a son or daughter, immediately begins the process of progressive sanctification, and after death will finally undergo glorification.

Written out then, the *Ordo Salutis* I have put forth looks like this –

1) gospel proclamation

2) conviction of sin

3) effectual calling

4) regeneration

5) faith/repentance[31]

---

[29] 10.1

[30] Sinclair B. Ferguson, *The Holy Spirit: Contours of Christian Theology* (Downers Grove, IL: InterVarsity Press, 1996), 132.

[31] In my previous book, *From Death to Life*, I addressed faith and repentance in greater depth. Since that is not the primary focus of this book, I've listed them together for the sake of brevity. "[R]epentance is the other side of saving faith. Coming to Christ in faith will always involve repentance of sin. As clear as we must be about the necessity of repentance, we don't repent to get to Christ. We come to Christ in saving faith and, in so doing, we repent…The sinner doesn't merely turn *away* from sin but he turns *to* Christ alone as his only suitable and all sufficient Savior. It is our turning to Christ that leads us to turn away from sin." Allen S. Nelson IV, *From Death to Life: How Salvation Works* (Conway, AR: Free Grace, 2018), 75.

6) justification

7) adoption

8) sanctification

9) glorification

As I alluded to above, I do not mean to present this as a "perfect" list. It is missing a few key components. A proper *Ordo Salutis* would have *unconditional election* at the beginning. It could also include *preservation* and *perseverance*. It might also label 5) as "conversion" since converting to Christianity is the person's volitional choice to believe on Christ and repent from his or her sins. Of course, this conversion flows from regeneration, which is one reason why thinking through the *Ordo Salutis* is so important.

Another glaring element missing is this list is *union with Christ*. Where should it go? Martyn Lloyd-Jones writes, "Logically, union [with Christ] should be put first, but not chronologically. We are regenerated because of our union with Christ; it is from Him we derive our life; it is from Him we derive everything."[32] As David VanDrunen helpfully reminds us, the *Ordo Salutis* should not be thought of as a "deistic process in which God knocks over the first domino...and the rest of the soteriological blessings tumble over in turn. Instead, each and every one is a blessing of Christ by his Spirit."[33]

Thus, "steps" 3-7, effectual calling, regeneration, faith, justification, and adoption are undoubtedly unique blessings flowing from Christ. Still, we must avoid separating these into their own distinct moment of time. A hyperbolically bad example would be to say, "I was effectually drawn (called) on Sunday, regenerated on Monday, had faith on Tuesday, was justified on Thursday, and adopted on Friday."

---

[32] David Martyn Lloyd-Jones, *God the Holy Spirit* (Wheaton: Crossway, 1997), 106.

[33] Matthew Barret, ed. The Doctrine on Which the Church Stands or Falls: Justification in Biblical, Theological, Historical, and Pastoral Perspective (Wheaton: Crossway, 2019), 502.

This is particularly important when discussing regeneration and faith. Regeneration precedes faith as a biblically mandated theological arrangement rather than as a moment in time. Thus, the Norman Geisler idea that regeneration preceding faith means we are "saved in order to believe" is nonsense.[34] We are not regenerated and then believe 0.003 seconds later. Instead, regeneration produces faith as the sun produces light.

We are regenerated, we believe, and are saved in that order. Hence, God works in our salvation in a logical and orderly way. Understanding how these pieces fit together properly has huge practical ramifications, as this book seeks to demonstrate regarding the proper place of regeneration.

Therefore, it helps to establish upfront what the biblical process of salvation looks like and where the subject of this book, regeneration, fits in. Hopefully, you see that it is impossible to discuss regeneration without also considering its proper place within the *Ordo Salutis*. Therefore, though we will inevitably touch upon other aspects of the *Ordo Salutis*, the focus is mainly on what it means to be born again and why a biblical understanding of this reality matters practically.

DEFINING A CHRISTIAN

We are now ready to conclude this chapter by giving a more formal definition of what constitutes a Christian. A Christian is *someone in union with Christ, who has been born again through the supernatural and mysterious work of the Holy Spirit by means of the gospel; and this regenerating work has resulted in his or her volitional (willing) belief in Christ and repentance from sin resulting in a life that desires to follow the Lord Jesus in every conceivable area.*

By grace alone, through faith alone, the ungodly one has been forgiven of all sin—past, present, and future—and is completely reconciled to God, having been fully justified before God.

---

[34] David L. Allen, Eric Hankins, and Adam Harwood, eds. *Anyone Can Be Saved: A Defense of "Traditional" Southern Baptist Soteriology* (Eugene, OR: WIPF & Stock, 2016), 80.

All of this has been accomplished by Jesus alone (Rom. 4:5) and the believer has now been given "the right to become [a child] of God" (John 1:12).

Furthermore, a Christian has been "delivered…from the domain of darkness and transferred…to the kingdom of [Christ]" (Col. 1:13). He has been transformed in such a way that he now lives a comprehensive life of repentance and faith and freely loves Christ, His people, His church, His ways, and His Scriptures. The Christian now longs to follow Jesus and obey Him in all things, great and small.

Some may think my definition too long. You may simply say something like, "A Christian is someone who has turned from their sins and believed the gospel of Christ." But I have sought to show that without one being born again – without a genuine change of heart – there is no Christian. This change of heart ultimately belongs to the Lord (cf. Jonah 2:9), for left to ourselves, we would continue to hate God (Rom. 8:7-8).

I have also endeavored to tip my hat here to the fact that regeneration is a massive overhaul that results in a total change. This change manifests itself in lifelong faith and repentance, evidenced by one's good works. We will get to all of that in due time.

For now, we are not quite finished understanding the nature of the human heart. Whenever you really want to get the details on your heart, the doctor will do a little bit of family history. This we will consider now as we take a brief historical survey of the doctrine of regeneration. Understanding our past will help us better assess the present in order to cut a better way forward for our future in understanding the doctrine of regeneration and why it matters.

3
FAMILY HISTORY

One of the things a good doctor will ask for when checking up on the health of your heart is your family history. The history of your family's hearts might give your physician critical insight into how to best treat you. History is certainly not everyone's cup of tea. But sometimes it can be a matter of life or death!

Similarly, in theology, understanding the past can help us accurately chart a good course for the future. Sadly, evangelicals seem to either not like their history or are just oblivious to where we came from. So, in this chapter I want to do a very brief sketch on a historical understanding of regeneration. I want to check our family's heart history, if you will.[35] The purpose of this chapter is not to get bogged down into historical details but to show us what others have believed and taught about regeneration and how the past continues to positively and negatively impact churches today.

---

[35] The objective of this book is not so much to build a historical case for understanding regeneration a certain way. I do think it is important, though, to highlight a few thoughts regarding regeneration from church history.

ANTE NICENE

The Nicene Creed first came about in 325 A.D. and states that the Holy Spirit is "the giver of life." The Ante-Nicene (not *Anti* Nicene) period is the time *before* 325 A.D. And though we do not find a robust systematic theology of the doctrine of regeneration, we do have some helpful thoughts regarding what it means to experience the second birth and its effects.

For example,

- In the 2nd century, Justin Martyr said of his own regeneration: "[S]traightway a flame was kindled in my soul; and a love of the prophets, and of those men who are friends of Christ, possessed me."[36]
- Tertullian, born c. 150 A.D., wrote, "Every soul, then, by reason of its birth, has its nature in Adam until it is born again in Christ; moreover, it is unclean all the while that it remains without this regeneration; and because unclean, it is actively sinful."[37]
- In the 3rd century, Cyprian of Carthage said, "[B]y the agency of the Spirit breathed from heaven, a second birth had restored me to a new man."[38]

I share these quotes simply to say that early Christianity understood the spiritual work which must come upon a soul to bring about transformation. This is in line with Paul's words in 2 Corinthians 5:17, "Therefore, if anyone is in Christ, he is a new creation. The old has passed away; behold, the new has come." Christianity is not an addendum to one's life. It is new life (cf. John 10:10).

---

[36] Justin Martyr, "Dialogue of Justin with Trypho, a Jew," in *The Apostolic Fathers with Justin Martyr and Irenaeus*, ed. Alexander Roberts, James Donaldson, and A. Cleveland Coxe, Vol. 1, The Ante-Nicene Fathers (Buffalo, NY: Christian Literature Company, 1885), 198.

[37] Tertullian, *A Treatise on the Soul*, Chapter 40. Accessed: https://www.newadvent.org/fathers/0310.htm.

[38] Elliot Ritzema, *300 Quotations for Preachers from the Early Church*, Pastorum Series (Bellingham, WA: Lexham, 2013).

AUGUSTINE VS. PELAGIUS

The Ante-Nicene period is certainly important, but it was the 5th century controversy in the church between Augustine and Pelagius that had an enormous impact on the church's understanding of regeneration. Pelagius essentially argued in such a way that would minimize the necessity of regeneration. He taught against being guilty because of Adam's sin, and against the corrupted nature we have because of sin (more on total depravity in the next chapter). In the Pelagian view, people have the ability to simply choose not to sin and are justified by *merit* instead of *grace*.

Pelagius had a problem with Augustine's statement, "Give what Thou commandest—and command what Thou wilt."[39] Augustine was acknowledging the necessity of God's grace to follow Him, while Pelagius overemphasized free will, saying, "God is [the will's] helper [only] whenever it chooses good."[40] That is like saying, "God helps those who first help themselves."

Unfortunately, during this time, many people understood baptism as the primary means of regeneration, which is not biblical (more on this in the coming chapters). But what Augustine did explain rightly was the idea of the effectual call of God. That is, if a person comes to Christ, it is because of the Spirit's sovereign work in calling and regeneration.

Augustine taught that coming to Christ or refusing Christ was an act of the human will. If man did not come, he was justly guilty for refusing Christ. If a man did choose to come, it was only because of efficacious grace. The ones God sovereignly calls to come to Christ actually come.[41]

---

[39] J.D. Douglas, "Pelagius," ed. J.D. Douglas and Philip W. Comfort, *Who's Who in Christian History* (Wheaton: Tyndale House, 1992), 546.
[40] Augustine of Hippo, "A Work on the Proceedings of Pelagius," in *Saint Augustin: Anti-Pelagian Writings*, ed. Philip Schaff, trans. Peter Holmes, Vol. 5, A Select Library of the Nicene and Post-Nicene Fathers of the Christian Church, First Series (New York: Christian Literature Company, 1887), 186.
[41] Augustine, "A Treatise on the Grace of Christ, and on Original Sin," in *Saint Augustin: Anti-Pelagian Writings*, 223.

Augustine understood that God works upon the sinner through effectual grace in such a way that the sinner responds by willfully and joyfully believing on Christ for his or her salvation. In contrast, Pelagius remained adamant that spiritually dead, unregenerate persons are able to respond positively to Christ whenever they decide for themselves to embrace grace. These two positions are mutually exclusive. They cannot both be biblical.

When I contemplate Augustine's thoughts on effectual calling, I think about the example of Lydia in Acts 16. In verse 14, Luke writes, "One who heard us was a woman named Lydia, from the city of Thyatira, a seller of purple goods, who was a worshiper of God. The Lord opened her heart to pay attention to what was said by Paul." That opening of the heart was God effectually drawing Lydia to Christ, resulting in her being born again and believing upon Jesus for her salvation. She did nothing to earn it; it was a gift from God.

Augustine was right. Regeneration is a work of sovereign grace alone. It is true that if a man does not come to Christ, it is because he does not want to. His *ability* to respond positively to the gospel has been corrupted by sin. The lost man's so-called "free" will has determined it will never bow the knee to King Jesus.

Therefore, we must emphatically maintain that lost people actually *do* respond to the gospel apart from any aid by the Holy Spirit. The problem is that their response is always rejection. Their wants and desires are set away from God. They cannot, nor do they desire to, respond positively to Christ, in and of themselves. Hence, as Augustine rightly explained, if anyone ever responds positively to Christ, it is only because of His effectual grace.

THE PURITANS AND EARLY EVANGELICALS

I'm going to skip the Middle Ages and the Reformation. Not because I don't think they are important, but if I don't watch myself, I'll make this whole book about church history. My goal is not church history as much as to encourage you to deepen your thinking about this precious doctrine of regeneration.

FAMILY HISTORY

The Puritans had a robust understanding of regeneration—maybe too robust, in a sense, because they labored quite extensively to tease it out into various aspects, which sometimes resulted in a long list of steps. That's not necessarily wrong, but I do want to reemphasize here the biblical understanding that regeneration is accomplished in a moment in time. It's not a process.

To be clear, the Puritan understanding of the doctrine of regeneration is helpful medicine to today's sickness of easy-believism.[42] These men were excellent at teaching that regeneration is God's work in man rather than God's work with man. Joel Beeke summarizes their teaching by writing, "There is no cooperation or synergism when it comes to regeneration. Man is not born of the Spirit *and* of his own will."[43]

I like to say that sinners do not come to Christ with a free will so much so as they do with a freed will because of God's initiating work in regeneration. I think the Puritans would accept that. Indeed, they taught that coming to Christ was a voluntary decision, but what caused a person to decide to come to Christ in saving faith was God "planting new habits in the will, whereby it is enabled to turn to God."[44]

The Puritans were also adamant that regeneration resulted in a total change. For example, Charnock wrote that the "new birth is necessary in every part of the soul."[45] The Puritans understood that

---

[42] "Easy-believism is a watered-down view of salvation that comes from a low view of God and a high view of man. The notion is that [true] repentance is not necessary for salvation, and all that is required by God is a simple decision to 'accept Jesus into your heart'…With this low view of God, God does not demand any more from us than a simple prayer, which is often accomplished by repeating the words of the pastor after walking to the front of the church. At best, the preacher may remind us at the last second that we need to repeat the sinner's prayer from the 'heart.'" Jeffrey D Johnson, *The Church: Why Bother?* (Birmingham, AL, Solid Ground, 2015), 20.

[43] Joel Beeke, *A Puritan Theology: Doctrine for Life* (Grand Rapids: Reformation Heritage, 2012), 470.

[44] Charnock, *A Discourse of the Efficient of Regeneration*.

[45] Stephen Charnock, *The Complete Works of Stephen Charnock*, Vol. 3 (Edinburgh; London; Dublin: James Nichol; James Nisbet and Co.; W. Robertson; G. Herbert, 1864–1866), 26–27.

it was not just part of a man that needed to be born again, but since sin had reached every corner of a person's heart, mind, and soul, his regeneration must also extend to the whole man. To put it more succinctly, since depravity is total, God's work of grace in regeneration must likewise be total.

I once heard Paul Washer tell the story of a friend who had asked the late Arnold Dallimore, "Dr. Dallimore, since the Puritans didn't give invitations, how did they know someone was saved?" Dallimore responded with, "That's easy. Because their life changed, and they continued to come to church." The Puritans understood that regeneration transformed the sinner.

From the Puritan era, let's move about 100 years later into the early evangelical movement. This formally introduces us to men like George Whitefield (1714-1770) and Jonathan Edwards (1703-1758). While Whitefield was passionately preaching, "You must be born again!" Edwards was writing a book called, *The Religious Affections*. In this work he argued that the work of the Holy Spirit brings about genuine religious affection in regeneration.

Edwards wrote, "Affections that are truly spiritual and gracious, do arise from those influences and operations on the heart, which are spiritual, supernatural and divine."[46] He went on to say,

> [T]he work of the Spirit of God in regeneration is often in Scripture compared to the giving a new sense, giving eyes to see, and ears to hear, unstopping the ears of the deaf, and opening the eyes of them that were born blind, and turning from darkness unto light. And because this spiritual sense is immensely the most noble and excellent, and that without which all other principles of perception, and all our faculties are useless and vain; therefore the giving this new sense, with the blessed fruits and effects of it in the soul, is compared to a raising the dead, and to a new creation.[47]

---

[46] Jonathan Edwards, *A Treatise Concerning Religious Affections: In Three Parts* (Oak Harbor, WA: Logos Research Systems, Inc., 1996), 65.
[47] Edwards, *Religious Affections*, 71.

In God's kind providence, it was a biblical understanding of the great doctrine of regeneration that birthed the evangelical movement of the 18th century and saw widespread revival in both the American colonies and across the Atlantic in England, Wales, and Scotland.

JACOB ARMINIUS AND JOHN WESLEY

I said I would skip the reformation era, but I cannot talk about Whitefield's and Edwards's contemporary, John Wesley (1703-1791) without briefly mentioning Jacob Arminius (1560-1609). Arminius wrote, "No one believes, without the exercise of his will. But the actual exercise of the will to believe is a different thing from the ability to will to believe; the latter belongs to all men, the former to the regenerate only, or rather to those enlightened by the grace of the Holy Spirit."[48]

Initially, this may not sound so bad. But what Arminius means is that all men are able to believe on Christ in and of themselves. They only need the assistance of divine grace to activate this belief. He wrote to early Puritan William Perkins, "You say that no grace is sufficient for conversion, which is not efficacious. I deny it...[I]t always remains in the power of the free-will to reject the grace bestowed, and to refuse subsequent grace."[49]

As an aside, the early 17th century Canons of Dort responded to the Arminian understanding of regeneration by writing that regeneration "is evidently a supernatural work, most powerful, and at the same time most delightful, astonishing, mysterious, and ineffable."[50] In a clear refutation of Arminius, the Canons go on to state, "Whereupon the will thus renewed is not only actuated and influenced by God, but in consequence of this influence becomes itself active. Wherefore also man himself is rightly said to believe and repent by virtue of that grace received."[51]

---

[48] James Arminius, *The Works of Arminius*, trans. James Nichols and W. R. Bagnall, Vol. 3 (Auburn; Buffalo: Derby, and Miller; Derby, Orton and Mulligan, 1853), 485.
[49] Arminius, *Works*, 511, 509.
[50] *Canons of Dort*, Article 12.
[51] *Canons of Dort*, Article 12.

Thus, the Canons of Dort, in opposition to Arminianism, articulated an understanding of a regeneration that effectually produced repentance and faith.

PREVENIENT GRACE

Not everyone, of course, embraced the teaching of the Canons of Dort. And this brings us back to John Wesley who chose, instead, to build upon the shaky soteriological foundation of Jacob Arminius. Wesley took Arminius's concept of God's work in regeneration and labeled it "prevenient grace."[52]

According to this system, God's grace can help a man come to Christ if he so chooses for it to help him. "But this grace is resistible, which accounts for some people choosing to believe in Christ and other people choosing not to."[53] Wesley, therefore, differed significantly from Whitefield and Edwards in his understanding of God's work in regeneration.

In the Wesley/Arminian system, then, regeneration is actualized by faith. After hearing the gospel, every person has some measure of grace by which he or she can activate his or her faith and believe in Christ, which in turn produces regeneration. Consequently, being born again is a combination of grace *and* the will of man.

The pivotal, decisive, crucial factor in the Wesley/Arminian system is man's choice on whether he wants to be born again or not. The Spirit moves first, of course, but at any point, a sinner may decide to reject or accept His grace. Sinners are dead in their trespasses and sins and then, through prevenient grace, made alive to see whether or not they want to be made alive or remain dead in their trespasses and sins.

---

[52] Francis X. Gumerlock, "Review of Prevenient Grace: God's Provision for Fallen Humanity by W. Brian Shelton," ed. Brandon D. Crowe, *Westminster Theological Journal*, Vol. 77, no. 2 (2015), 437.

[53] Kirk R. MacGregor, "Regeneration," ed. John D. Barry et al., The Lexham Bible Dictionary (Bellingham, WA: Lexham, 2016).

So, in this errant system, being born again is not *ultimately* of grace alone. Rather, in the end, man determines whether he will use that grace in order to believe. The Arminian/Wesleyan understanding of regeneration is both unbiblical and seriously damaging to this and other areas of Christian life and doctrine.

CHARLES FINNEY

Arminian and Wesleyan theology is incredibly problematic, but it only worsens with "the most influential revivalist of the later stages of the Second Great Awakening", Charles Grandison Finney (1792-1875).[54]

When you hear the name, Charles Finney, you should cue ominous music in your head. In his own way, he is even worse than Pelagius because he took the false teaching of Pelagianism and sought to make it more palatable. Instead of getting rid of the poison, he decided he'd just add a spoonful of sugar to help the heresy go down. Then he marketed it like a mad-man.

Here is an example of Finney's preaching from John 3:7,

> Regeneration, then, must consist in something in which man's will is something more than passive. It is true, as I shall have occasion to remark, that in regeneration man is a recipient, and a passive recipient, if you will, in a certain sense, of the divine influence; but this divine influence, instead of superseding man's own agency, is only employed in bringing about that change by his own agency, which constitutes regeneration.[55]

Did you catch that? Like Arminius and Wesley, Finney argues that being born again occurs only in response to human decision. Man is passive in regeneration *after* he decides he wants it.

---

[54] Kidd, *America's Religious History*, 77.
[55] From Charles Finney's sermon, *Regeneration*. Accessed: http://www.revivaltheology.net/13_salvation/fregen.html.

According to Finney, God brings about the new birth subsequent to the sinner's change of mind. Essentially, the sinner sees the kingdom of God, wants it, and in exchange, God grants him regeneration. But Jesus says, "Truly, truly, I say to you, unless one is born again he cannot see the kingdom of God," (John 3:3).

Our Lord's teaching is why D. Martyn Lloyd-Jones, in stark contrast to Finney's thought, rightly said, "[R]egeneration is obviously something which is done by God...in which men and women are entirely passive and contribute nothing, nothing whatsoever." Lloyd-Jones could not be any clearer. Regeneration, "is something that happens to us; we are begotten, we do not beget ourselves, we cannot generate ourselves. It is entirely the work of God in us and upon us."[56]

That which is born of the flesh is flesh (John 3:6). The flesh or will of man simply cannot bring about regeneration (John 1:12-13). We are entirely passive in regeneration rather than cooperating with God or initiating the process.

We might term Finney's understanding of regeneration as "decisionalism." Tom Nettles summarizes Finney's view using his own words. "The sinner himself is the final effective agent of change and 'is, therefore himself, in the most proper sense, the author of the change.' Finney emphasized relentlessly, 'God commands you to do it, expects you to do it, and if it ever is done, you must do it.'" In the final analysis, according to Finney, "The sinner himself finally produces 'the actual turning, or change.'"[57]

Nettles goes on to summarize Finney's view, writing, "Regeneration, therefore, is 'something over which we have control, for which we are responsible.' It consists of the 'supreme ultimate intention of the soul,' a change of character resulting from an 'executive volition' producing a 'benevolent ultimate choice.'" Finney could not be any more emphatic when he says, "'Regeneration then is a radical change of ultimate intention...'"[58]

---

[56] Lloyd-Jones, *God the Holy Spirit*, 82–83.
[57] Robert Gonzales Jr., ed., *The Confessing Baptist: Essays on the Use of Creeds in the Baptist Faith & Life* (Conway, AR: Free Grace, 2021), 81.
[58] Gonzales, *The Confessing Baptist*, 82.

Much of what we see today in evangelicalism is a rehash of Charles Finney-ism. Since all that separates God and man is a "decision" to love, follow, trust, and obey Christ – which a person is said to be able to make while having an unregenerate heart – all sorts of emotive and in some cases even manipulative means may be employed in order to push the sinner over the edge to choose Jesus. Sadly, many churches still employ such hollow means of "getting people saved."

Decisionalism would say that it is not the removal of a stone heart one needs but only the prompting of influential argumentation. Or, worse, if one wants to be born again, then he or she ought to just change their own heart! All a preacher needs to do is to convince a rebellious, spiritually dead sinner to desire regeneration, and then God will grant it. God will move if we will first decide that's what we want Him to do.

Think about this though. If you have the power to move toward God, why do you even need regeneration at all? If you can obey the Lord's command to repent and believe the gospel (Mark 1:15) by your own power, why do you need to be born again? Why can't you just pull yourself up by your own bootstraps and work hard in your own strength to live the Christian life?

As Lloyd-Jones notes, "If I have already got the ability and the power and the discrimination to recognise truth and to desire it, then I do not need to be regenerated. But the fact is, of course, that I do not have such a power."[59] We, therefore, like Jesus said, must be born again.

THE 21ST CENTURY

I happened to watch a clip of a Paul Washer sermon one evening with my family. In that sermon, I remember he said that "the most forgotten doctrine in the church today is the doctrine of regeneration." I think he's probably on point with his assessment. And if regeneration is not the *most* neglected doctrine, it's up

---

[59] Lloyd-Jones, *God the Holy Spirit*, 89.

there somewhere near the top of the list. A misunderstanding and underemphasis of this doctrine of regeneration has contributed to the unraveling of evangelicalism in the 21st century.

Through the continued influence of Pelagius, Arminius, Wesley, Finney, and our own sinful pride decisionalistic methodology continues to be utilized today. Will Metzger nails it when he writes, "Well-meaning Christians have adopted easy formulas leading many into easy-believism and cheapening grace."[60]

Decisionalism is unbiblical and ultimately sets the grace of God aside as something not desperately needed. Furthermore, it also results in all sorts of present-day tomfoolery (instead of relying upon God's grace in the gospel) to manipulate a person into making a decision for Christ. Whether it's gimmicks on stage, free t-shirts, just saying God loves you over and over, or diluting the gospel altogether, when we minimize the doctrine of the new birth, we find ourselves in a mess.

The Bible says in Romans 1:16 that the *gospel* is the power of God unto salvation. When a sinner is brought to Christ, it is the result of the grace of God in the gospel. That's why we must preach the gospel. We must rely on the gospel to change sinners' hearts. It is imperative we return to this reality in the 21st century.

CONCLUSION

We have sought in this chapter to provide a brief historical survey of some of the key definitions and theories of regeneration in the church. In no way do we put church history on the same level as the Scriptures. Yet, it is important to consider what those who have gone before us believed in order to help us study the Scriptures and to aid us in carefully thinking through the precious doctrine the Bible presents us.

We want to both glean from the good of those who have gone before us and learn from the error of others. I want to be clear that

---

[60] Will Metzger, *Tell the Truth: The Whole Gospel to the Whole Person by Whole People* (Downers Grove, IL: InterVarsity, 2002), 41.

misunderstanding regeneration does not necessarily make one an unbeliever. What we see in church history and what we will see in Part III of this work, is that a proper understanding of regeneration has massive ramifications on the Christian life in numerous areas.

Now we'll move back from church history to return to Jesus's confrontation with Nicodemus in John 3. Revisiting this dialogue moves us into Part II of this book where we seek to dive deeply into the nature of regeneration. And in order to help our understanding of what regeneration is, we will begin by considering why it is needed.

Why is it that one *must* be born again? We seek to answer that question in the following two chapters as we discuss the necessity of regeneration.

PART II

WHAT IT MEANS TO BE REGENERATED (BORN AGAIN)

4
YOU *MUST* BE BORN AGAIN: THE NECESSITY OF REGENERATION (PART I)

Autonomy is the idol of the 21st century. We desire to be independent of all authority. Children reject parental commands. Employees balk at their boss's instruction. Multitudes seek to change their God-given gender and/or shout "My body, my choice!" Sadly, it is our sinful, human nature to seek independence from the God who made us. Like our first parents, we want to be like God (Gen. 3:5). All of this is why Jesus says, "You *must* be born again" (John 3:7).

From a broader perspective, we must not be tempted to minimize doctrine given our current cultural climate. Not that there is *ever* a time to reduce doctrine, but in the darkest of days the church must shine forth the truth all the more brightly. In the pitch-black night, do you want a cheap flashlight or do you want something that's going to burn your retinas if you stare into it? You want a spotlight! The church must endeavor to shine all the more brightly during seasons of significant darkness and peril.

YOU *MUST*

Revisiting John 3:7, Jesus says to Nicodemus, "Do not marvel that I said to you, 'You must be born again.'" Note the words, "You must." The word "you" here is plural. D.A. Carson notes, "The plural 'you' sets Jesus over against not just Nicodemus, but the entire human race."[61] In other words, this teaching isn't just for our friend, Nick. It's for everyone. It is a universal reality.

Then we have the word "must." This is a word of necessity. If anyone is to see the kingdom of God (John 3:3), he or she *must* be born again. This is non-negotiable. As J.C. Ryle preached, "we must each of us between the cradle and grave go through a spiritual change, a change of heart, or in other words be born again; and in the text you have heard read the Lord Jesus declares positively, without it no man shall see the kingdom of God."[62]

When Jesus says, "You must be born again," He's not giving us a good idea or merely good advice. He's not opening up an opportunity for us to negotiate a counteroffer. To see the kingdom of God, being born again is a *must*. It is a *requirement*. Jonathan Dickinson preached this truth to the American Colonies, "We must become new creatures, or perish eternally."[63] If anyone is to become a Christian, he or she must be born again.

The question we want to answer now is, Why? Why must a person be born again? Why is it so non-negotiable that a person be born again to become a Christian? Is God just trying to make things more difficult for us? We need to begin answering this question by addressing the sinner's problem.

---

[61] D. A. Carson, *The Gospel According to John*, Pillar New Testament Commentary (Leicester, England; Grand Rapids: InterVarsity; W.B. Eerdmans, 1991), 197.
[62] J. C. Ryle, *The Christian Race and Other Sermons* (London: Hodder and Stoughton, 1900), 16.
[63] Richard Owen Roberts, ed. *Salvation in Full Color: Twenty Sermons by Great Awakening Preachers* (Wheaton: International Awakening, 1994), 136-137.

THE PROBLEM

I think an exegetical key to understanding Jesus's words in John 3:7 is returning to the end of John 2. Remember that when the Biblical authors were writing the Scriptures, they did not give them chapter divisions. So, I think considering the end of John 2 is an important lead-in to understanding all that's happening in John 3.

John 2:23-25 says, "Now when he was in Jerusalem at the Passover Feast, many believed in his name when they saw the signs that he was doing. But Jesus on his part did not entrust himself to them, because he knew all people and needed no one to bear witness about man, for he himself knew what was in man."

This immediately precedes the interaction with Nicodemus, so I think it is a vital tool in helping us understand this dialogue. Remember, the chapter and verse divisions are not inspired by the Holy Spirit and came much later. While chapters and verses are helpful, they are not infallible.

What happens is that sometimes you run into a verse or a chapter that ends or begins in a funny place. I think the end of John 2 is an example of that. Perhaps it would have been better for our understanding of this interaction with Nicodemus if John 3 really began at John 2:23.

That fact that Jesus knows what was in man connects directly to what He says to Nicodemus in John 3:7, "You must be born again." You see, there were people who believed in Jesus, but, apparently, it wasn't saving belief, was it? How do we know? Because, "Jesus on his part did not entrust himself to them." Why? "For he himself knew what was in man."

What was in man? Sin. Rebellion. Love of self. Jesus did not entrust Himself to sinners who put forth a superficial belief. By the way, this word for "believe" is the same word used in John 3:16. One type of "believing" saves and one type of "believing" does not save. And the difference is, where does this belief originate? If it originates within man, it is superficial because of sin.

John 3:1-8 precedes John 3:16 as a compelling reminder that true and saving belief flows from the Spirit's work in the grace of regeneration. This is not to be understood as though the Holy Spirit believes *for* us, but that He enables us to believe. More on that in a later chapter.

Frankly, mankind underestimates both the putridness and consequences of sin. This is true even within evangelicalism, and the results are disastrous to our theology and methodology. Martyn Lloyd-Jones once preached, "A light view of sin always leads to a superficial salvation and to a superficial Christian life."[64] If we minimize sin and its effects, then we minimize the purpose and power of the gospel. Ultimately, we minimize the glory of King Jesus.

Jesus teaches us more about the effects of sin in John 6:63, "It is the Spirit who gives life; the flesh is no help at all." We see here a problem for sinners. And that is, the flesh is no help at all in bringing spiritual life.

If we convert that into percentages, we could say it this way: the flesh helps 0%. As the King James Version says, "the flesh profiteth nothing." The flesh contributes nothing to our being born again, and the Holy Spirit does 100% of the work.

Now, what is "the flesh"? What Jesus means here is that by your own human effort, you *cannot* have spiritual life. No man can bring about his own regeneration. One will not have new life simply by hearing or seeing or touching. Merely saying, "I believe in Jesus," doesn't cut it. Something else must happen. The Holy Spirit must give life.

The sinner's problem is one of *inability*. This is why Jesus says in John 6:44 and 6:65 that no one has the *ability* to come to Him unless granted by the Father. Why is this?

Sin has tainted absolutely everything about us—even our will. The inclination of our soul is not toward Christ but away from Him.

---

[64] D. Martyn Lloyd-Jones, *Born of God: Sermons from John, Chapter One* (Carlisle, PA: Banner of Truth Trust, 2011), 32.

Our hearts have the opportunity to bow to Christ or to self as the ultimate king of our lives. Apart from the effectual working of the Holy Spirit, we choose self every time.[65]

This is why Jesus told the Jews in John 5:40, "you *refuse* to come to me that you may have life." *Refuse* in that verse is translated from two Greek words. The first is οὐ, meaning "not." The second is, θέλετε, meaning "willing." Jesus is saying the reason His audience would not come to Him for eternal life is because they were "not willing."

As John Gill notes of John 5:40, "such [was] the depravity, perverseness, and stubbornness of their wills, that they had no inclination, desire, and will to come to Christ, any more than power."[66] People are willing to continue on in their sin and rejection of Christ. They are not willing to come to Christ for salvation.[67]

Since the Fall of Man, humanity has inherited both the guilt and sin nature of Adam in such a way that everything about us is affected by sin. Two quick Scripture references will suffice here. In Genesis 6:5, God says of mankind that, "every intention of the thoughts of his heart was only evil continually." Now, perhaps you think that is only an antediluvian condition. But in Genesis 8:22 *after* the Flood, the Lord says, "the intention of man's heart is evil from his youth."

TOTAL DEPRAVITY

So, yes, Jesus knew what was in man all right: an unbelieving heart, a heart set on evil, a heart that seeks to serve self above all others—even our Creator. This condition of the heart is one symptom of

---

[65] For a discussion on natural and moral ability see Herman Bavinck, *Reformed Dogmatics*, Vol. 3 (Grand Rapids: Baker Academic, 2006), 121-122.

[66] John Gill, *An Exposition of the New Testament*, Vol. 1, Baptist Commentary Series (London: Mathews and Leigh, 1809), 808.

[67] The Auburn Declaration of 1837 states, "While sinners have all the faculties necessary to a perfect moral agency and a just accountability, such is their love of sin and opposition to God and his law, that, independently of the renewing influence or almighty energy of the Holy Spirit, they never will comply with the commands of God." Philip Schaff, *The Creeds of Christendom, with a History and Critical Notes: The Evangelical Protestant Creeds, with Translations*, Vol. 3 (New York: Harper & Brothers, 1882), 779.

what theologians call total depravity or radical corruption. This does not mean every person is as sinful as they could possibly be. It does mean that every part of a person has been corrupted – the heart, mind, will, affections, desires, critical thinking, everything (see, for example, Isa. 59:3, Jer. 17:9, Ps. 53:1-3, Matt. 15:19, Rom. 3:10-18, Rom. 8:7-8, Eph. 2:1, John 8:34, John 3:19).

Tom Ascol notes,

> As has been well said, the heart of the human problem is the problem of the human heart. Not the blood pumping vessel that is the concern of your cardiologist, but the seat of your personality that is the concern of the Gospel. Jesus teaches us that there is something far more fundamental to our sinfulness than the actual sins we commit. Our sins do not make us sinful. Rather, we commit sins because, at the very center of our lives, we are sinful. Sin has invaded the inner recesses of our personalities.[68]

Thus, we begin to see a clearer picture of Jesus's words to Nicodemus in John 3:7. Being born again is a necessity because the human heart is evil. Notice that Jesus tells Nicodemus not to marvel at this truth. That word, marvel, can mean, "wonder" or "amazement." Sometimes it is translated in other places as "astonished."

However, Nicodemus should not have been astonished. His study of the Scriptures should have helped him understand the great gap between God and man. Nicodemus should not have been surprised at "the need for a God-given new birth, and God's promise that he would give his people a new heart, a new nature, clean lives and a full measure of the Spirit on the last day."[69]

What Jesus reveals to us here *is* astonishing to too many evangelicals today. He is saying that the human heart is so steeped in sin that, without regeneration, no person will ever believe on Him savingly. Without the new birth, no one has true spiritual life or the effects that follow that spiritual life. Regeneration is essential for a person to savingly embrace Christ and live for His glory.

---

[68] https://founders.org/2020/06/18/the-heart-of-the-problem/
[69] Carson, *The Gospel according to John*, 197.

You may have heard thousands of sermons telling you how good you are, how worthy you are, and how, if you'll just try Jesus, God will be so excited to finally have you on His team. In contrast, our Lord teaches in John 3 that your heart is in such an immoral and depraved state that your only hope is for it to be transformed. Without this happening, you won't ever savingly believe on Christ.

NECESSARY TO BELIEVE

In the last sermon he ever preached, John Bunyan said, "Believing is the consequence of the new birth."[70] We've already noted Jesus's words in John 6:63. To further substantiate this truth, we turn to John's first epistle. To build our case, we will examine 1 John 2:29, 3:9, 4:7, and finally, 5:1. Take note of the repeated phrase in each verse in italics.

- "If you know that he is righteous, you may be sure that everyone who practices righteousness *has been born* of him." (1 John 2:29, emphasis mine)

- "No one born of God makes a practice of sinning, for God's seed abides in him; and he cannot keep on sinning, because he *has been born* of God." (1 John 3:9, emphasis mine)

- "Beloved, let us love one another, for love is from God, and whoever loves *has been born* of God and knows God." (1 John 4:7, emphasis mine)

- "Everyone who believes that Jesus is the Christ has been born of God, and everyone who loves the Father loves whoever *has been born* of him." (1 John 5:1, emphasis mine)

The Apostle John writes to reveal to his readers the fruits of being born again. First, he shows that practicing righteousness is a fruit (manifestation) of being born again (1 John 2:29). Next, he shows that avoiding sin is a fruit of being born again (1 John 3:9). Thirdly, he shows that love of the brethren is a fruit of those who have been born again (1 John 4:7).

---

[70] John Bunyan, *Bunyan's Last Sermon*, Vol. 2 (Bellingham, WA: Logos Bible Software, 2006), 756.

To summarize, a holy life, fighting sin, and loving God and the brethren are not things one does *in order* to be born again but because he *has been born* of God. These characteristics occur *because* of regeneration. In other words, regeneration is not the *effect* of these acts but the *cause*. As Benjamin Keach (1640-1704) wrote, "You… must act from Life, and not for Life."[71] The acts John mentions are not *for* life, but flow *from* new life.

What I have just written is not controversial to any conservative Bible-believing Christian. No one is making grammatical arguments for why John might really mean that practicing righteousness *precedes* regeneration. However, when we get to 1 John 5:1, things get a little controversial.

This is not because John has changed his style. He uses the same grammatical construction in 1 John 5 that he has used in chapters 2, 3, and 4. The problem for some is that now he has said everyone who *believes* – the same word for "belief" in John 3:16 – *has been* born of God.

Grammatically, "has been" in any of these 1 John verses could be simply translated "is," like it is in the NASB or the KJV in 1 John 5:1. Thus, one might make the argument that it does not matter to John in this verse which comes first – belief or regeneration.

Am I making a mountain out of a mole hill? Absolutely not! I would argue that his whole purpose in writing this epistle is to show certain evidences of regeneration so that Christians can know that they are saved (cf. 1 John 5:13). John's epistle gives us the assurance we treasure and take comfort in.

Therefore, righteousness, a practice of right living, love, and faith flow *from* regeneration rather than being the *cause* of regeneration. We do not give God any of these things in order to earn our place in heaven. Instead, we do them *because* we have been given spiritual life.

Some theologians get so focused on the grammar of 1 John 5:1 – present participles and perfect tense verb combinations – that they miss the central purpose of John's writing. That is, some so ardently

---

[71] Benjamin Keach, *The Marrow of True Justification, Or, Justification without Works* (London: Dorman Newman, 1692), 37.

oppose regeneration preceding faith that they miss the bigger picture of what John is doing in his letter.[72] The Apostle is showing what those born of God look like – they practice righteousness, they do not practice sinning, they love God and the brethren, and they believe on Christ.

When we understand the purpose of the Apostle John's writing as a whole, we will agree with what John Piper says of 1 John 5:1, "New birth precedes and is the enabling power behind our faith."[73] I like this statement because it presents us with a test of sorts. Suppose what Piper says about 1 John 5:1 is correct (and I am arguing that it is). In that case, it should also work with 1 John 2:29, 3:9, 4:7 since they are similarly constructed and part of the Apostle John's overarching argument for his epistle.

Let's take a moment and try this out. We will use Piper's original statement and replace the word "faith" with what 1 John 2:29, 3:9, and 4:7 say:

- New birth precedes and is the enabling power behind our *practicing righteousness* (2:29)
- New birth precedes and is the enabling power behind our *not practicing sinning* (3:9)
- New birth precedes and is the enabling power behind our *love for fellow believers* (4:7)

When we examine these verses in this manner, we see that this is precisely what the Apostle is communicating. Whatever you say of one of these statements in 1 John 2:29, 3:9, 4:7, and 5:1, you need to be able to say of them all.

This is how Charles Spurgeon can say of 1 John 5:1, "[T]his faith, wherever it exists, is in every case, without exception, the gift of God and the work of the Holy Spirit....

---

[72] See, for example, David L. Allen, "Does Regeneration Precede Faith?," *Journal of Baptist Theology and Missions 11*, no. 2 (2014), 41.
[73] John Piper, *Look at the Book Labs* (Minneapolis: Desiring God, 2014–2015), 1 Jn 5:1–4.

Faith is too celestial a grace to spring up in human nature until it is renewed; faith is in every believer 'the gift of God' (Eph 2:8)."[74]

Man's will, whether it's in righteous deeds or saving faith, does not move the Spirit of God. The Spirit of God moves (*frees*) man's will (John 3:8). Our natural, sinful unwillingness and hostility to Jesus, and all things righteous, necessitates being born again for any person to savingly believe on Christ.

REJECTING TOTAL DEPRAVITY

Not everyone wants to accept the idea of total depravity or radical corruption presented in this chapter. This idea of man's *inability* to cooperate with the grace of God by participating in his own salvation is contrary to our pride. We want to say we somehow help God help us. We don't. God is responsible for 100% of our salvation—and all of it through His grace and mercy.

The 2012 "Statement of the Traditional Southern Baptist Understanding of God's Plan of Salvation" says in Article 2, "We deny that Adam's sin resulted in the incapacitation of any person's free will." In other words, the framers of this statement seek to uphold the Wesleyan idea of synergism. This is a popular view in a large segment of evangelicalism today.

Basically, this concept asserts that there is enough good in man to decide for himself whether he will do the right thing or not in cooperating with God to bring about his regeneration. This is a widespread view among evangelicals today, *but it is not the biblical view.*

Here are three reasons why total depravity is rejected:

1. *It presents a low view of man:*

Human nature loves to be coddled. It loves to be encouraged. Men and women love to be told of their self-worth, self-importance, and innate goodness. This biblical view of sin and inability destroys all of that. Rather than presenting mankind as deserving people

---

[74] Charles Spurgeon, *Spurgeon Commentary: 1 John*, ed. Elliot Ritzema, Spurgeon Commentary Series (Bellingham, WA: Lexham, 2014), 1 John 5:1.

worthy of God's grace, Scripture shows that men, women, boys, and girls are not only undeserving but actually worthy of the eternal wrath of God. To say, "You *must* be born again" is astonishing to the sinful soul, but when we examine the biblical evidence, it shouldn't be astonishing at all.

God does not gush over us like a high school crush but "has bent and readied his bow" because "If a man does not repent, God will whet his sword" (Ps. 7:12).

2. *It grates against human experience:*

Another reason this idea of sin and inability is rejected is that it seems to contradict what we experience in everyday life. That is, we all know unbelievers whom we would refer to as "good" people. They pay their taxes, volunteer at the homeless shelter, and seem to be moral, upstanding citizens.

Unbelievers can do "good" things. It's good to teach children math. It's good to dig water wells in Africa. It's good to pick up litter. But none of these things constitute righteousness before God, because none of the good things unbelievers do proceed from faith (cf. Heb. 11:6). These acts are all evil in the sense that they are done from a desire for autonomy and from a heart of rebellion against a good and holy God. John Owen properly analyzes the issue when he writes, "A religious, decent, moral life, derived from self and not 'born of God' is as sinful as the worst of sinful lives."[75]

3. *It requires a radical solution:*

Total depravity means that no person will ever believe on Christ without the gracious regenerating work of the Spirit of God. Man is so incapacitated by sin that the only way his desires for Christ and heaven will be holy and righteous is if the Spirit of God works efficaciously in his heart.

Thomas Manton preached, "A man's heart is where his love is."[76]

---

[75] Sinclair B. Ferguson, *The Holy Spirit: Contours of Christian Theology* (Downers Grove, IL: InterVarsity Press, 1996), 132.

[76] Thomas Manton, The Complete Works of Thomas Manton, Vol. 13 (London: James Nisbet & Co., 1873), 178.

And the unregenerate heart has no love for the holy things of God. The radical solution required is that one must be born again before he or she will truly seek Christ.

NO NEUTRALITY

Loraine Boettner writes that all "[Unbelievers] possess a fixed bias of the will against God, and instinctively and willingly turn to evil."[77] The only hope for the dead rebellious heart of every human being is that it would be brought to life by the power of the Holy Spirit under the heralding of the gospel of Jesus Christ.

Men, women, boys, and girls are so lost in sin, so in love with the world, so dismissive of all things holy and righteous that they are unwilling and unable to come to Christ for salvation on their own. People freely choose what they want to do every single day. But, as R.C. Sproul articulated, "Our wills are such that we cannot freely choose what we have no desire to choose. The fundamental loss of a desire for God is the heart of original sin. The lack of desire for the things of God renders us morally unable to choose the good."[78]

This does not mean lost men and women never have any desire to go to heaven. It is possible to see within a lost person an inclination toward heaven or even to live for the Lord. As the saying goes, "there are no atheists in foxholes." People often make deals with God in order to get out of or into a specific situation.

But upon closer examination, these deals are really about self-perseveration or "fire insurance." Lost persons have no holy desire to enjoy the glories of Christ or to bring honor to His name, but only to avoid temporal pain or to gain material pleasure—things like getting a raise or winning a ballgame or being rescued from a battle. To these people who view God as a genie in a bottle, God is there for them and not the other way around.

---

[77] Loraine Boettner, *The Reformed Doctrine of Predestination* (Phillipsburg, NJ: P&R, 1991), 62.

[78] R.C. Sproul, *What is Reformed Theology? Understanding the Basics* (Grand Rapids: Baker, 1997), 135.

Others may desire heaven in order to avoid the agonies of hell or to experience a blissful eternity with friends and family members. For these, their desire for heaven has nothing to do with the glory of God and everything to do with their own comfort. Many would claim they are neutral on the subject of Christianity. They have nothing *against* Jesus. They just don't believe all that stuff. They believe it's possible to sit on the fence when it comes to salvation—they are not for or against it.

However, a lost person's will is *not* neutral. No matter how nice that person is, according to the Bible, his will is evil and stubborn (Jer. 7:24). It is enslaved to sin (John 8:34, Rom. 6:17). Apart from the grace of God, no one is "good." It is immoral to disobey and disbelieve the Bible since it is God's breathed-out Word. It doesn't matter how shiny someone's life may appear on the outside, those who do not love God are immoral wretches in need of, but not deserving of, God's grace.

Certainly, lost persons make decisions every day. But these decisions are never holy decisions because the unregenerate will does not have the ability to make holy decisions since it is in bondage to sin.[79] "The flesh profiteth nothing."

Unregenerate people aren't in the prison of sin wanting to be rescued. In one sense, the prison door is wide open, but they rather stay in their cold cell. They love the darkness. They love evil. They love to break God's Law. Essentially, lost people love their faux autonomy. They desire to be a god unto themselves and turn their backs on the One True God of heaven (cf. Rom. 3:10-18).

Now, you say, "Well, if one cannot come to Christ apart from God's grace why even preach the gospel?" For one thing, we've been commanded to. That's good enough, right? But the second and more important reason is this: God's grace operates through the heralding of His gospel (James 1:18). We will pick up these themes more in Chapter 6. But for now, we need to spend one more chapter on the necessity of regeneration.

---

[79] Boettner, *The Reformed Doctrine of Predestination*, 62.

5
THE NATURAL MAN: THE NECESSITY OF REGENERATION (PART II)

My wife and I have five children. I can say that with each child's arrival, I never got over the wonder of birth. This tiny human enters the world experiencing things like she never has before. Birth is an amazing and beautiful gift of God.

Jesus uses the analogy of our physical birth in His dialogue with Nicodemus for a reason. A person could never do anything without first being born. The same holds true of the necessity of our second birth. This is why Jesus says, "unless one is born again he cannot see the kingdom of God," and "Do not marvel that I said to you, 'You must be born again'" (John 3:3,7).

In the last chapter, we sought to increase our understanding of the depth of sin and its effects on mankind. Martyn Lloyd-Jones preached, "It is true of man not only that is he in the dark, but that the darkness is also in him."[80] There is no neutrality when it comes to Jesus. No one can sit on the fence on this issue. You either belong to Jesus or you don't.

---

[80] Lloyd-Jones, Born of God, 26.

Experientially, this may be hard for us to fathom because we run into people all the time who profess to love Jesus. And maybe even in their minds, they think they do. Or if they do not love Him, at least, they don't hate Him.

But this isn't the biblical teaching. Roman 8:7-8 says, "For the mind that is set on the flesh is hostile to God, for it does not submit to God's law; indeed, it cannot. Those who are in the flesh cannot please God." John 3:20 says, "For everyone who does wicked things hates the light and does not come to the light, lest his works should be exposed." And in John 7:7, Jesus says the world *hates* Him.

There is no neutrality when it comes to Jesus. If neutrality was possible, then perhaps we could talk about those neutral people not needing to be born again. However, it is not possible. In reality, all are hostile to God, and all need to be born again. Because this is such a hard truth for so many to swallow, we are going to spend another chapter discussing the absolute necessity of being born again.

UNABLE TO UNDERSTAND

Paul writes in 1 Corinthians 2:14 that "the natural person does not accept the things of the Spirit of God, for they are folly to him, and he is not able to understand them because they are spiritually discerned."

The natural man. This is like when Jesus says that which is flesh is flesh. The flesh produces flesh. Natural people produce natural people. The natural person is the person not born again. That person does not accept the things of God. They are folly to him.

Take a moment and read 1 Corinthians 1:18-27. This word for folly is used six times in that passage to demonstrate that for the natural man, the unregenerate man the things of Christ are *foolishness.* In some cases, the natural man may appear to cling to Christ and even tell others he is clinging to Christ, but in his heart of hearts the things of God are silly. He does not like them and, if he were honest, he would tell you they seem absurd to him. All this stuff about propitiation, atonement, the gospel—it's all ultimately foolishness to the natural man.

THE NATURAL MAN: THE NECESSITY OF REGENERATION (PART II)

He is *unable* to understand them because they are spiritually discerned. This is the same word for ability used in John 6:44, 65. Paul says the sinner does not have the *ability* to understand the cross in his own power.

With this in mind, let's back up to see the surrounding context of 1 Corinthians 2:14—1 Corinthians 2:12-15:

> [12] Now we have received not the spirit of the world, but the Spirit who is from God, that we might understand the things freely given us by God. [13] And we impart this in words not taught by human wisdom but taught by the Spirit, interpreting spiritual truths to those who are spiritual. [14] The natural person does not accept the things of the Spirit of God, for they are folly to him, and he is not able to understand them because they are spiritually discerned. [15] The spiritual person judges all things, but is himself to be judged by no one.

We see here that Paul is contrasting the natural man and the spiritual man. The natural man does not care about the things of Christ. They are folly to him. He doesn't understand them. Again, it is not as though the natural man desires Christ but God won't let him come. Rather, it is all foolishness to him.

Charles Hodge notes, "[M]an in the highest development of his nature, can neither discover 'the things of the Spirit,' nor receive them when revealed. It is of God, and not because of their superior culture or refinement, that men are in Christ." [81]

In contrast to the natural man, the spiritual person, then, does understand and therefore loves Christ. What is the difference? The Spirit of God has efficaciously influenced him, and he has been given "a divine supernatural knowledge."[82]

---

[81] Charles Hodge, *An Exposition of the First Epistle to the Corinthians* (New York: Robert Carter & Brothers, 1857), 42.
[82] Richard Sibbes, *The Complete Works of Richard Sibbes,* ed. Alexander Balloch Grosart, Vol. 4 (Edinburgh; London; Dublin: James Nichol; James Nisbet and Co.; W. Robertson, 1863), 161.

The other is hardened by his own sin and moved by the spirit of the world. That brings me to my next passage.

THE VEILED GOSPEL

In his second epistle to the Corinthians, Paul writes,

> ³ And even if our gospel is veiled, it is veiled to those who are perishing. ⁴ In their case the god of this world has blinded the minds of the unbelievers, to keep them from seeing the light of the gospel of the glory of Christ, who is the image of God. ⁵ For what we proclaim is not ourselves, but Jesus Christ as Lord, with ourselves as your servants for Jesus' sake. ⁶ For God, who said, "Let light shine out of darkness," has shone in our hearts to give the light of the knowledge of the glory of God in the face of Jesus Christ. (2 Cor. 4:3-6)

Not only is the sinner unable and unwilling to come to Christ. Not only are the things of Christ folly to him. But also, here, we see that Satan blinds unbelievers from seeing the glory of Christ. Satan keeps them from seeing the truth. But it's not as though they're looking for it. Rather, their own unwillingness gives way to Satan blinding them to leave the unregenerate sinner in a very precarious and hopeless scenario, if he is depending upon his own power and good works to earn salvation.

Notice in 2 Corinthians 4:5-6 that Paul is once more contrasting the unbeliever and the believer. The difference is, yet again, the Holy Spirit. The affections of the lost man are turned inwardly on sin and self. And the affections cannot be altered from within. Something must happen from without. God must say, "Let there be light" in the hearts of His people. We must be born again. Regeneration is necessary for any person to become a Christian.

SPINACH AND BUZZARDS

I want you to think about spinach and a child, for example. Take a 7-year-old and put spinach in front of them. And then tell them:

"Hey, just love this, okay? Just make yourself love this spinach." That won't happen. That can't happen. That little girl simply cannot *will* herself to love something she hates.

So too with the religious affections. A person cannot merely say, "Okay, now I'm going to love Christ and the things of Christ." It won't happen. The things of Christ are folly to him, and the god of this world has blinded his eyes.

Let's take another example. Capture a wild buzzard and put rancid meat in front of him and a fresh salad. And say, "Hey, don't choose the squashed possum. Choose the Caesar salad. Don't love the rancid meat! Love the salad!" (Never mind that you are now talking to buzzards.)

What will he do? He's a buzzard. He will act in accordance with his nature. He will choose the roadkill. That roadkill smells heavenly to him. That's who he is. Who unbelievers are, apart from Christ: dead in trespasses and sins, according to Ephesians 2:1. They suppress the truth in unrighteousness, according to Romans 1:18. They do not seek after God or understand, according to Romans 3:11.

For unbelievers to come to Christ, they need their minds changed. They need their hearts changed. Their wills changed. Their affections changed.

Yet, this is how too many people present Christianity: You must do the things you hate to do and not do the things you really want to do all in an effort to make it to heaven.[83] But biblical Christianity is that we need to be *born again*. We need new life. We need God to remove our heart of stone and replace it with a heart of flesh. It is only from that supernatural act that we look to Christ in faith, repent of our sins, trust Christ, rest in Christ, love Christ, and desire to walk after Christ. Without a new sense, new eyes, and new ears we will never run to Christ in saving faith.[84]

In a way, those who are perishing have a problem they don't even recognize. They love the world. They love their carnal appetite.

---

[83] I first heard this example in a Paul Washer sermon.
[84] Edwards, *Religious Affections*, 71.

They love fleeting pleasure. They love sin. And on top of all that, Paul says the god of this world blinds them. They hate the idea of Christ ruling over them. They want nothing to do with Jesus or true religion.

RELIGIOUS MOTIONS ≠ RELIGIOUS AFFECTIONS

The sinner may go through the motions of religion. We think of Judas, for example. Or what about Esau, even? "For you know that afterward, when he desired to inherit the blessing, he was rejected, for he found no chance to repent, though he sought it with tears" (Heb. 12:17). Though Esau is in the Old Testament, he is an example of someone trying to outwardly conform to rules without a true change of heart.

It is true, then, that lost people sometimes merely go through the motions of religion. This is one reason Jonathan Edwards wrote his most famous book on *The Religious Affections*. During the Great Awakening there were some people who seemed to be converted, but later it turned out they were not.

By the way, this is why we must exercise caution when we hear that 500 people came forward at church camp or at the end of a revival service, or whatever. It wouldn't be helping them or the church, for us to simply declare, "They're all saved!" Instead, cautiously and prayerfully, we should counsel them well as we observe their lives. If their salvation is genuine, their lives will show their change of heart.

Edwards warned that people may start talking a lot about religious things. Or they may start coming to church every week. There may even be an appearance of love for God and His people in a person. But none of these outward behaviors guarantees that a person is truly a Christian.

Edwards writes, "He who has no religious affection, is in a state of spiritual death, and is wholly destitute of the powerful, quickening, saving influences of the Spirit of God upon his heart."[85]

---

[85] Jonathan Edwards, *The Works of Jonathan Edwards*, Vol. 1 (Carlisle, PA: Banner of Truth Trust, 1974), 243.

See, the sinner will go to great lengths, even deceiving himself, so as not to truly bow the knee to Christ and enjoy Him for who He is.

WILL YOU WALK AWAY?

The concept of human inability runs directly against human pride. Jesus contrasted these in John 6 and was met with a great departure of so-called disciples. I imagine if any of his disciples were church-growth gurus, they had to be frustrated with his tactics. Consider the event from the end of John 6.

Jesus said, "'It is the Spirit who gives life; the flesh is no help at all…This is why I told you that no one can come to me unless it is granted him by the Father.' After this many of his disciples turned back and no longer walked with him" (John 6:63a, 65-66).

I don't think Jesus's teaching on human inability is necessarily everything that caused these disciples to leave, but it is a significant contributor. In other words, lost persons do not want to hear about the sinner's inability. And they haven't been wanting to hear it for a very long time – even in the days of Jesus, from the mouth of Jesus Himself.

There is a greater problem out there than global warming, worldwide pandemics, or inequality, and that is sin. Unless we are born again, we will not see the kingdom of God. Society has such an idolatrous love of human autonomy that we don't want to admit our need or inability.

This is how serious our pride problem is: These people were listening to Jesus in the flesh. They were in the physical presence of the King. They had seen His miracles. They had not long before eaten of the bread and fish! They had heard His teaching. But then Jesus attacked their pride and sense of self-autonomy. And they walked away. "Many *of his disciples* turned back and no longer walked with him."

Men are so prideful and so in love with the thought of their own self-sufficiency that even if Jesus Himself stands in front of them and tells them of their inability, they won't listen. They will walk away.

This is the power of our affections. It is our affections that move our wills so to speak. It's one thing for the soul to understand something, but it's quite another for the soul to be inclined toward something or will to do something.

Marriage provides a good illustration. Your wife doesn't just want you to help pick up the house. She wants you to *want* to help clean up the house. She doesn't want you to take her out on a date because you feel obligated to do so. She wants you to *want* to take her out.

Many people understand the gospel. Many people could pass a seminary exam on justification by faith alone. Many people walk through the doors of a church building every Sunday. But it's one thing to *understand* what the Bible says. It's quite another to genuinely desire to live accordingly with holy aspirations.

HOW TO ATTEND THE THINGS OF CHRIST

I've observed three wrong ways for people to attend to the things of Christ—things like prayer, and Bible intake, sharing Christ, coming to church, and pursuing holiness. Without a heart that has been changed by the Holy Spirit, this is what their service looks like:

1. Drudgery – I know I should be doing these religious things, but I don't really want to. But, I guess I'd better because I want to go to heaven.
2. Pharisee – I'm doing these things, so God loves me more and more. I'm not perfect but I'm better than that guy and I deserve some blessings because of all the good I do.
3. Apathy – I don't care. I've been saved and the preacher told me to write it in my Bible so I'm good. I don't care about attending to the things of Christ

People in all three of these scenarios understand what they are supposed to do. But they don't want to attend to the things of Christ for the glory of God and the true blessedness of their souls. Their foolish hearts are still darkened. Mere lip service doesn't please Almighty God.

THE NATURAL MAN: THE NECESSITY OF REGENERATION (PART II)

Christians live for Christ *because* we've been born again, not *in order to* be born again. Going through the motions of Christianity without any genuine religious affection for Christ, for the people of Christ, for the glory of Christ indicates a person who is blinded, deceived, hardened, and dead in his trespasses and sins (Jer. 17:9, Eph. 2:1ff, Mt. 15:19).

In and of ourselves we cannot and will not choose Jesus (John 6:44, 63). The natural man does not love God, fear God, understand God, or have anything to do with following God (1 Cor. 2:14, Rom. 3:10-18). This is why regeneration is necessary. This is why we must be born again!

We have taken two chapters to explore the sinner's inability and the absolute necessity of being born again. The question we now come to is: if the sinner can't do it, who can? In other words, if our wills are inclined away from Christ and our affections are corrupted and centered on self, how does that change? Is there any hope for the lost soul?

Unquestionably, the answer is yes. What is impossible with men is possible with God (Luke 18:27). Being born again is grace upon grace. We needed to understand our inability so that we can understand God's grace in regeneration.

In our next chapter, we will explore God's *sovereignty* in regeneration. Just as we saw God stoop down to the first lifeless man in Eden and breathe into Him the breath of life, so too does the Holy Spirit, of His own sovereign initiative, come upon spiritually lifeless sinners and cause them to live.

6
MONERGISM: GOD'S SOVEREIGNTY IN REGENERATION

In the movie, *The Princess Bride,* the protagonist, Westley dies. Or does he? In this particular scene, Inigo Montoya says to Miracle Max about Westley, "He's dead. He can't talk." But Max responds with, "Look who knows so much! It just so happens that your friend here is only mostly dead. There's a big difference between mostly dead and all dead."

Well, Max is right. There is a big difference between dead and mostly dead. As Miracle Max says, himself, "Mostly dead is slightly alive." However, when it comes to the spiritual condition of the human race, there are only two categories: alive or dead. "Mostly dead" doesn't exist.

John Owen wrote, "All men can be divided into two groups. They are either regenerate or unregenerate."[86] There is no third way. There is no middle ground. Ernest Reisinger agreed, writing, "There are no degrees in regeneration – a man is regenerate or he is not."[87]

---

[86] From John Owen's book on the Holy Spirit. Cited from https://www.monergism.com/effectual-operation-blessed-spirit-regeneration-or-conversion-sinners.
[87] Ernest C. Reisinger, *Today's Evangelism: It's Message and Methods* (Phillipsburg, NJ: Craig, 1982), 51.

How then does a spiritually dead man come to life? Seeing how others have come to Christ is an encouragement to believers. Let's begin this chapter by looking at four conversion testimonies from church history. I want you to notice something in common with each of these testimonies below. It is one thing to "study" the doctrine of regeneration, but it is another to see it happen to an individual.

JOHN WESLEY

Back to our old friend John Wesley. Perhaps you are a bit surprised that I chose him. True, I do disagree with Wesley on several important doctrinal points. But I chose him for two reasons. First, I think we will see him in heaven. Secondly, his experience of being born again was better than his theology of regeneration.

On May 24, 1738, Wesley reluctantly went to a meeting where someone was reading Martin Luther's preface to Romans. Sometime around 8:45pm, something changed. Wesley writes, "I felt my heart strangely warmed. I felt I did trust in Christ, Christ alone for salvation, and an assurance was given me that he had taken away my sins, even mine, and saved me from the law of sin and death."[88]

Before this time, John Wesley had been a member of the Holy Club at Oxford, where he and the most serious of his classmates went to great lengths to practice holy and moral lives. He had been on a missionary journey to Savannah, GA, in 1735. Outwardly, Wesley was doing everything right. But inwardly, his heart was dead and cold. So that night on May 24, 1738, he listened to someone reading Luther's preface to Romans, and he felt his heart "strangely warmed."

CHARLES WESLEY

Similar to his brother John, Charles outwardly lived a righteous life. Inwardly, his heart was rotten. He dated his regeneration a few days before John on May 21, 1738. In the providence of God, Charles had fallen ill and picked up a copy of Luther's commentary on Galatians.

---

[88] Mark Galli and Ted Olsen, *131 Christians Everyone Should Know* (Nashville: Broadman & Holman, 2000), 182.

Feeling his heart cold, he began to pray. A couple of days later he wrote the lines of this hymn describing God's Work in his soul,

> Long my imprisoned spirit lay,
> Fast bound in sin and nature's night;
> Thine eye diffused a quick'ning ray—
> I woke, the dungeon flamed with light;
> My chains fell off, my heart was free,
> I rose, went forth, and followed Thee.[89]

AUGUSTINE OF HIPPO

We talked a bit about Augustine's theology in chapter 2. Consider now how he came to Christ. In 386, after much prayer from his mother and many talks with and sermons by his friend Ambrose, God breathed spiritual life into Augustine.

Augustine found himself sitting outside under a tree one day, crying because of conviction of sin. He then heard a neighbor child chanting, "Take up and read; take up and read." This caused Augustine to spring up and run to his Bible, opening to Romans 13:13-14 which says, "Let us walk properly as in the daytime, not in orgies and drunkenness, not in sexual immorality and sensuality, not in quarreling and jealousy. But put on the Lord Jesus Christ, and make no provision for the flesh, to gratify its desires." Augustine writes, "No further would I read; nor needed I: for instantly at the end of this sentence, by a light as it were of serenity infused into my heart, all the darkness of doubt vanished away."[90]

JOHN BUNYAN

Sometime in the early 1650s, after a long struggle of sin and conviction and trying to be a Christian, John Bunyan was born again. He notes that as he walked along the road one day, his conscience was pricked about the state of his soul. He then began to think of

---

[89] Galli and Olsen, *131 Christians,* 158.
[90] Augustine, *Confessions,* Book VIII. Accessed: https://www.gutenberg.org/files/3296/3296-h/3296-h.htm.

the phrase, "Thy righteousness is in heaven", which he would later conclude came from 1 Corinthians 1:30. It was this phrase that helped him finally see that God does not accept our own righteous deeds, but rather Christ's in our stead.

It was then that Bunyan recounts, "Now did my chains fall off my legs indeed, I was loosed from my affliction and irons, my temptations also fled away; so that, from that time, those dreadful scriptures of God left off to trouble me; now went I also home rejoicing, for the grace and love of God."[91]

THE TAKEAWAY

Of course, we see some differences in each of those testimonies, but we also see significant similarities. And as far as we are able to tell, each one is a genuine testimony of one being born again. Notice one thing missing in each of those testimonies is someone praying a prayer to receive Christ or asking Jesus into their heart. That is a modern invention. That wasn't used until maybe the mid-1800s at the earliest—and largely due to Charles Finney's heretical influence and practice.

I don't mean to insinuate if we've prayed that prayer that we aren't saved. I've prayed that sinner's prayer myself. *But I wasn't born again because of it.* And many, sadly, are falsely assured of their salvation based on saying that prayer but having no change of heart or life.

In each of these men listed above, we see that the Word of God was involved in some way. We see that the change brought about was lasting. We also see that they did not choose the time and place of their conversion. That is the subject of this chapter. God is sovereign in bringing about regeneration when He will for whom He will.

YOU MUST *BE*

Let's go back to our conversation between Jesus and Nicodemus in

---

[91] John Bunyan, *Grace Abounding to the Chief of Sinners*, Vol. 1 (Bellingham, WA: Logos Bible Software, 2006), 35–36.

John 3. We have already focused on the word "must" in discussing the necessity of regeneration. Now I want to look at the two English words that follow– "You must *be born*" (John 3:7, emphasis mine).

Jesus isn't telling us what we must "do" in this text, but what we must "be." If Jesus had said "you must birth yourself" we would be in big trouble. Not only is that statement illogical as an illustration, but it is also impossible to do. You and I can't "birth ourselves," and because of our sin nature we would never want to!

As John Murray wrote, "If it were not the case that in regeneration we are passive, the subjects of an action of which God alone is the agent, there would be no gospel at all. For unless God by sovereign, operative grace had turned our enmity into love and our disbelief to faith we would never yield the response of faith and love."[92]

Similarly, though perhaps a bit more strongly, Owen says, "To say that we are able by our own efforts to think good thoughts or give God spiritual obedience before we are spiritually regenerate is to overthrow the gospel and the faith of the universal church in all ages. It does not matter how powerfully we are motivated and encouraged, without regeneration we can do no good works which are pleasing and acceptable to God."[93]

Thus, regeneration is not a work performed by yourself and God. Instead, it is a work of God in you. We know, without a doubt, that this is Jesus's meaning because there is no better illustration He could have used than "birth." A person does not will their first birth (or their conception).[94]

Benjamin Keach makes this point when he writes, "A Child may as easily beget it self in the Womb before it self was, as a Man can form Christ in his own Soul, or regenerate himself; 'tis God that

---

[92] John Murray, *Redemption Accomplished and Applied* (Grand Rapids: Eerdmans, 2015), 104.
[93] https://www.monergism.com/thethreshold/articles/onsite/owenoverthrow.html
[94] There has been debate over whether the term γεννάω in John 3:3 means to "birth" or "conceive," but either way the point stands. A person has zero control over their first birth or conception.

doth it, the Holy Spirit begets us."[95] A person cannot cause their first birth (physically), nor can they cause their second (spiritually). This is the point Jesus makes here.

Hercules Collins, a contemporary of Benjamin Keach in the 17th century, said it this way: "[I]n regeneration man is wholly passive, and can contribute no more to his being a new creature than his being a creature in the first place. Wherever regeneration is wrought, it is the pure product of God's eternal will, and not of the creature's: 'Of his own will begat he us' (Jam 1:18)."[96]

Collins brings up another important passage, James 1:18, showing that our regeneration is tied to God's eternal will rather than our own. Or consider Ephesians 2:4-5, "But God, being rich in mercy, because of the great love with which he loved us, even when we were dead in our trespasses, made us alive together with Christ—by grace you have been saved…"

When does God make us alive? *Even when we were dead in our trespasses.* There is a moment when we are dead and passive. Passive, actually, is not the most precise word. We are actively *opposed* to God. Yet, it is in that very state that God is the actor upon us. It is while we are dead in our sins that God gives us life. This is God's sovereignty in regeneration.

THE MERCY OF GOD

Another passage to consider in God's sovereign regenerating work is 1 Peter 1:3-4a, "Blessed be the God and Father of our Lord Jesus Christ! According to his great mercy, he has caused us to be born again to a living hope through the resurrection of Jesus Christ from the dead…"

Peter wrote in Greek, but to understand his point, we need to consider the Hebrew word, *"chesed."* This word is often translated as "steadfast love" (in the ESV), but might be better understood as

---

[95] Benjamin Keach, *A Golden Mine Opened* (London, 1694), 212.
[96] Hercules Collins, *Mountains of Brass*. See: https://www.chapellibrary.org/read/mobr (Chapter 2, G).

"covenantal love," or "loyal love." It's quite a pregnant word full of comfort for the Christian.

It's used 249 times in the Old Testament—129 times in in the Psalms alone. It appears in Isaiah 54:8, which says, "'In overflowing anger for a moment I hid my face from you, but with everlasting love (*chesed*) I will have compassion on you,' says the LORD, your Redeemer" (emphasis mine).

In Psalm 136, this word is used 26 times, once in each verse. Psalm 136 ends this way in verse 26, "Give thanks to the God of heaven, for his *steadfast love* endures forever." Psalm 63:3 says, "Because your *steadfast love* is better than life, my lips will praise you."

When Greek writers wanted to convey *chesed*, they would usually use the Greek word *eleos*, translated in the New Testament as "mercy" (Luke 10:37, Rom. 9:23, Jude 1:21, etc.). In the Greek version of the Old Testament, the Septuagint, both Isaiah 54:8 and Psalm 136[97] use the Greek word *eleos* to translate the Hebrew word *chesed*. So does Palm 63:3.[98] This Greek word for "mercy" is used to communicate the Hebrew understanding of Yahweh's loyal covenantal steadfast love.

It is proper for us, then, at times, when we see the word for mercy used in the New Testament, to understand a connection with the Hebrews concept of *chesed*. That's what we have going on in 1 Peter 1:3. The way we are born again is by God, and the reason He does this is because of His loyal covenantal steadfast love. Peter understood the concept of *chesed*. He understood the Greek Septuagint.

Therefore, it is not a stretch to conclude that Peter is communicating this Hebrew idea of *chesed* to us by the Greek phrase, "great mercy." The Apostle emphasizes more than mere mercy, but an eternal, sovereign, loyal, faithful, covenantal love. We are born again according to God's steadfast love. We owe our lives to God's mercy. The cause of our regeneration does not originate in us but from the incalculable depths of God's abundant mercy.

---

[97] This is Psalm 135 in the Septuagint.
[98] This verse is Psalm 62:4 in the Septuagint.

There is nothing in us to bring about our new birth. In fact, all that is in us – sin – demands justice. We are not neutral and in hope of God showing us a bit of kindness. Instead, we are rebellious by nature and choice, and in desperate need of great mercy.

Oh, the hope we have in mercy! One prayer from *The Valley of Vision* puts it beautifully. "All things in me call for my rejection, All things in thee plead my acceptance."[99] Not because of what is in man, but according to His great *mercy*, the Triune God redeems sinners.

The Father elected a people to redeem, the Son perfectly accomplished this redemption, and the Spirit applies this redemption through the proclamation of the gospel. The Trinity works in beautiful harmony in the salvation of God's people for God's infinite glory.

Through what Jesus has done—His perfect life, substitutionary death, His burial, and resurrection— sinners are made new by the merciful power of God alone. John Calvin writes,

> [S]upernatural life is a gift, because we are born the children of wrath; for had we been born to the hope of life according to the flesh, there would have been no necessity of being [born] again by God. Therefore Peter teaches us, that we who are by nature destined to eternal death, are restored to life by God's mercy… All, indeed, confess that God is the only author of our salvation, but they afterwards invent extraneous causes, which take away so much from his mercy.[100]

Calvin nails it. We cannot confess on one hand that God is the author of our salvation while on the other hand inventing "extraneous causes" that deny His necessary mercy. Regeneration is a consequence of the steadfast love and mercy of God alone.

---

[99] Arthur Bennett, ed. *The Valley of Vision* (Carlisle, PA: Banner of Truth, 2005), 150.
[100] John Calvin and John Owen, *Commentaries on the Catholic Epistles* (Bellingham, WA: Logos Bible Software, 2010), 28-29.

MONERGISM: GOD'S SOVEREIGNTY IN REGENERATION

You and I don't earn God's love. It is bestowed upon us by His free grace and great mercy. The regenerating work of God could never be earned or brought about by the will of man (cf. John 1:13). A proper, accurate, biblical understanding of regeneration causes Christians, from the depths of our souls, to give God all the glory for our salvation.

I am not born again because I am better than anyone else. I'm not born again because I am smarter than anyone else. I am not born again based on saying a prayer, responding to an altar call, or because I did 0.001% of the work. I am not born again because of me at all but sheerly because of mercy, God's glorious steadfast love. Being born again was ultimately God's choice for me rather than my choice for Him. Without regeneration, I would never have turned to Christ.

What if we changed the words of 1 Peter 1:3 a bit? What if we said, "according to our great wisdom, we caused ourselves to be born again"? Or what if we said, "we allowed God to cause us to be born again"? Or what if it said, "according to His great mercy, God helped us to be born again"?

First, that would be a repudiation of the Bible's plain wording. But what else would that do? It would increase man and decrease God. It would not give God the glory He deserves in His regenerating work in our lives.

The Bible is straightforward about God's initiating work in salvation as He draws us to Himself and causes us to be born again by the power of the Holy Spirit. This isn't something hidden in some obscure passage of Scripture. It's not relegated to the footnotes. It's everywhere!

Notice that we've now seen John, James, Peter, and Paul, all give us this same understanding of God's sovereign work in regeneration. Regeneration is a work of God in man. As R.C. Sproul rightly noted, "Only the Holy Spirit can change a heart."[101] So, how does this work?

---

[101] R. C. Sproul, *What Is the Great Commission?*, 1st Ed., The Crucial Questions Series (Orlando: Reformation Trust, 2015), 19.

THE USE OF MEANS

The first thing we want to affirm is the use of means. The Spirit works through the proclamation of the gospel. In each of those testimonies we considered above, every man was either hearing, reading, or meditating on the truths of the gospel.

The Holy Spirit uses the word of truth to bring us from death to life (cf. James 1:18). The Holy Spirit convicts the sinner, shows him or her their need for Christ, and then opens their heart to cry out to Christ in faith (like Lydia in Acts 16:14).

That introduces us to another area of emphasis. The relationship between regeneration and faith ought to be seen in terms of causation rather than in terms of time. An illustration of this is a light switch. What happens first? Does the light switch go on, or does the light come on? Well, temporally, that is, in time, it almost appears as though these happen simultaneously. There is no real gap. The switch goes up, and the light comes on nearly instantaneously from our perspective.

But we know that one causes the other. The light coming on doesn't cause the switch to go up. The switch being flipped up causes the light to come on. Now, that's just an analogy. But it's similar to regeneration and faith. Faith is not the cause of regeneration. Regeneration is the cause of faith.

Certainly, the Bible doesn't tell us to call to sinners to go be regenerated. Rather, it tells us to call sinners to believe on Christ. Why? That's man's responsibility. It is every man's duty to turn from his sin and believe the gospel. Men and women are called to choose Jesus. In fact, no one has ever become a Christian without choosing Jesus.

Am I contradicting myself? After telling you that salvation is 100% of God, am I now saying that you have to contribute something to your own conversion? By no means!

Do not out-think yourself here. Charles Spurgeon put it this way, "If you allow self-invented difficulties to keep you from accepting pardon through your Lord and Saviour, you will perish in a condemnation which will be richly deserved. Do not commit spiritual suicide through a passion for discussing metaphysical subtleties."[102] Or as John Flavel writes, "though faith be the gift of God, and the power of believing be derived from God, yet the act of believing is properly our act."[103]

The sovereignty of God does not take away from the responsibility or even choices of man. Jeff Johnson notes, "The elect are not forced to believe against their wills. Rather, God changes and renews and quickens their hearts so that they are willing in the day of His power (Ps. 110:3). Likewise, the reprobate are not prevented by God from coming to Christ."[104]

As we've seen then, both God's work and man's faith are required for a person to be a Christian. But what we are emphasizing in this chapter is that God's sovereign and gracious work comes first and is in such a way that it brings about the desired outcome. God sovereignly acts upon our heart, thereby giving us the desire and ability to choose Him. Without regeneration, we could not do this. Faith is a response to regeneration, not the basis for it.

Lost people will never choose Jesus in and of themselves because they are so in love with sin and self. Left to their own resources, they will reject Christ 100% of the time. Yet God, in His great mercy, graciously uses the preaching of the gospel, or a tract, or book about the gospel, or an evangelistic conversation, or simply reading or meditating upon the Scriptures; and through His word turns on the light.

There is no time gap. That person immediately, joyfully and willingly looks to Christ in faith, trusting in His finished work, and repenting of his or her sins. In that moment, they are immediately justified by grace through faith, and adopted as a son or daughter

---

[102] R. C. Sproul, *What Is the Great Commission?*, 1st Ed., The Crucial Questions Series (Orlando: Reformation Trust, 2015), 19.
[103] John Flavel, *The Whole Works of the Reverend John Flavel*, Vol. 6 (London; Edinburgh; Dublin: W. Baynes and Son; Waugh and Innes; M. Keene, 1820), 352.
[104] Johnson, *The Sovereignty of God*, 157.

of the Most High. The Bible is clear. You must be born again. Regeneration is not accomplished by man but given by grace.

- Regeneration is not achieved via a prayer.
- It is not achieved via baptism.
- It is not achieved via the Lord's Supper.
- It is not achieved via a moral life.

Regeneration is God's work in man through the heralding of the gospel. Since it is necessary for man to be born again, and since he or she is unwilling and unable to bring about their second birth just like they can't bring about their first birth, this is all God's doing.

It's like what Jesus says in Matthew 12:33, "Either make the tree good and its fruit good, or make the tree bad and its fruit bad, for the tree is known by its fruit." The sinner, the bad tree, needs something outside of himself if he is ever to be made good. When a sinner begins to produce good fruit, it is because the power of God has sovereignly changed his heart by the gospel.

SUPERNATURAL

Christianity is supernatural. Left to ourselves, we do not fear God, seek God, truly understand God, or care about God's glory at all. Without the Holy Spirit, we don't even want to know the problem, much less possess the means or the desire to fix it ourselves. A leopard cannot change its spots, and a sinner cannot change his nature (cf. Jer. 13:23).

So, how does anyone get saved at all then? With man, this is impossible! But God. God opens our hearts to understand the gospel. He breaks down the fortress of hostility we have erected to show us the wonders of His grace. God brings about a change of heart in us so that we come to Christ in faith and repentance.

As John MacArthur summarizes, "Regeneration is the cause, not the consequence of saving faith."[105]

Part III of this book explains five reasons why it's so important to have this biblical understanding of salvation's supernatural origin. Let's consider two other reasons now:

1. It gives all glory to God for our salvation.

Two big words need to be mentioned here. One is *monergism*, and the other is *synergism*. Ergon is the Greek word for work. The prefix *syn* means with, and the prefix *mono* means alone.

Therefore, the word "synergism" means that the new birth results from the work between God and man. It says the New Birth is God's work *with* man. God does His part; man does his part, and *voila!* – regeneration. This is a faulty concept. "Monergism," on the other hand, means that the new birth is God's work *alone*. And that's the accurate concept I've been arguing for, because *it is the biblical teaching*. Regeneration is God's work in man (not God's work "with" man).

Titus 3:5 says, "[H]e saved us, not because of works done by us in righteousness, but according to his own mercy, by the washing of regeneration and renewal of the Holy Spirit..." We did not save ourselves. We did not make ourselves savable. Rather, God saved us. As D. Martyn Lloyd-Jones preached, "[Y]ou do not become a

---

[105] John MacArthur and Richard Mayhue, ed. *Biblical Doctrine: A Systematic Summary of Bible Truth* (Wheaton: Crossway, 2017), 586. He also notes, "In his state of spiritual death (Eph. 2:1-3), man is incapable of even understanding the things of the Spirit, let alone receive them (1 Cor. 2:14). The sinner's mind is so hostile to God that he is literally unable to submit to God's law (Rom. 8:7), and thus he cannot please God in any sense (Rom. 8:8), including the exercise of faith (Heb. 11:6). Man is blind to the value of God's glory revealed in Christ and is hopelessly enamored with sin, despite its worthlessness. To suggest that a sinner in such a state could, apart from the regenerating grace of the Holy Spirit, summon from within his own deadness the saving faith that God declares to be his sovereign gift (Eph. 2:8) is to wholly underestimate the miserable nature of man's depravity."

Christian as the result of human activity, not even human endeavor at its best and highest…Becoming a Christian is all of God."[106]

Monergism states, "God caused us to be born again," while synergism says, "God helped us to be born again." Which is more faithful to the Scriptures? Which brings God the glory? "[O]nly monergism can do justice to the glory of God in salvation."[107]

2. It makes us dependent on God's means rather than our own.

As evangelical Anglican John Stott (1921-2011) wrote, "[H]uman beings cannot save souls. Only the power of God can give sight to the blind and life to the dead."[108] We must not rest in our power to convert sinners, for we have none. Rather, we must depend on the Spirit's power (cf. 1 Cor.2:4).

For example, as Christian parents, one of the biggest things we want is for our children to come to Christ. But instead of getting your kids to say a canned prayer, what I'm advocating is to depend on the Holy Spirit by continuing to share the gospel. Exposure to the word of truth is what they need. Faith comes from hearing![109]

Certainly, it is good to pray with them. And pray for them. Don't force them. Don't try to accomplish what you cannot control. We can control some things. We can control praying for them. We can control sharing the gospel with them and calling them to repent and believe it. We can control putting the Scriptures before their little eyes, singing faithful songs, talking about the things of Christ and His gospel.

And for the rest, trust the Lord. Trust the Lord to work through His appointed means – prayer, gospel proclamation, Scripture intake,

---

[106] Lloyd-Jones, *Born of God*, 233.
[107] Matthew Barrett and Thomas J. Nettles, eds. *Whomever He Wills: A Surprising Display of Sovereign Mercy* (Cape Coral, FL: Founders, 2012), 121.
[108] John Stott, *Basic Christian Leadership: Biblical Models of Church, Gospel and Ministry* (Downers Grove, IL: Intervarsity, 2002), 49.
[109] Romans 10:17 states, "faith comes from hearing, and hearing through the word of Christ." The Word of God is so practical in its instruction. But we must believe it.

and the local church. Do not grow weary in well doing with your children! (Galatians 6:9).

You see, some evangelists and preachers try to get kids or adults to pray something before they even understand what they're praying for. They don't understand the gospel. They don't understand repentance. They don't understand a desire to follow Christ. It's ridiculous to force them into an insincere mechanical prayer.

We've come to think we can magically create regeneration with words. But this is not true. You must "be" born again. This isn't what *we* do; it's what *God* does. Christianity is supernatural.

SAFER IN GOD'S HANDS

Though the inability of man to help save himself might be a difficult truth for sinful man to swallow, here is the glorious news: the Holy Spirit is pleased to bring undeserving sinners from death to life! And as John Bunyan preached, "To be saved by grace supposeth that God hath taken the salvation of our souls into his own hand; and to be sure it is safer in God's hand than ours."[110]

Oh, the new birth is certainly safer in God's hand than ours! We can trust our children's souls, our neighbors' souls, and the souls of the nations to a sovereign and gracious God. We preach, we pray, we plead, we persist. We take the gospel far and wide. All the while we trust God with the results for, "Salvation belongs to the Lord!" (Jonah 2:9). He will work for the glory of His name and the magnification of Christ.

Truly many will be left to their own fallen will to reject the glorious gospel of Jesus Christ and continue in their hardness of heart. God is not unjust to leave so many rebels to their own sins. But it will not be this way for all. God will work in His sovereign grace through the gospel in bringing many sons and daughters to glory.

Regeneration is the beginning of the Christian life brought about by God's sovereign grace. It is accompanied with faith that clings to

---

[110] John Bunyan, *Saved by Grace*, Vol. 1 (Bellingham, WA: Logos Bible Software, 2006), 354.

Christ. Furthermore, the sovereignty of God in regeneration means He brings about a complete overhaul of the man or woman resulting in lasting change. God transforms undeserving sinners. With this in mind, we now turn to the totality of regeneration.

7
REALLY NEW:
THE TOTALITY OF REGENERATION

Human beings are constantly subjected to changing conditions. Arkansans, for example, experience the "cold and heat, summer and winter" blessings of Genesis 8:22 sometimes all in a single day! The weather changes. The economy changes. Political platforms change.

These outward circumstances can bring good and bad effects to the world around us and even to our own level of happiness or frustration. But none of these external circumstances bring about deep change. Ultimately, we do not need more laws, policies, mandates, or referendums. The change we really need, the change all humanity stands in need of, is a change of heart. We need to be born again.

We've seen thus far that regeneration is necessary. And we've seen that it comes about sovereignly. It is God's work of free grace *in* us, not His work *with* us. Regeneration is not a team effort. And in this chapter, we want to examine its totality. That is, to be born again really and totally changes a person. He or she really becomes a new creation (cf. 2 Cor. 5:17).

THE BORN IDENTITY

We travel back again now to that encounter 2,000 years ago when a man of the Pharisees, Nicodemus, approached Jesus by night. We do not know his full intention for talking with Jesus, but we know he got more than he bargained for as Jesus told him of his need to be born again.

Eight times in the six verses of John 3:3-8 we read the word *born*. Jesus uses physical birth to illustrate spiritual birth. Jesus says, "You must be *born*..." As the old preacher once said, "I still haven't gotten over my first birth." Our first birth massively impacts us.

Now, we do not deny the personhood of babies still in the womb. But an amazing thing takes place during the first birth, doesn't it? It is why this day is called your "birth-day." It's the day everyone recognizes when you came into the world. It is the day by which we calculate your age.

Your first birth has impacted you tremendously. So much so that, if not for your first birth, you would not be reading this book right now. I don't mean to be funny here. I mean to set in context the illustration that Jesus is using. There is a reason He is using the language of being born to describe regeneration. If the first birth impacted you so much, how much more the second birth?

THE BORN (AGAIN) LEGACY

When the new birth occurs, the Christian becomes an entirely new creation and has been given new life. It is a true heart transformation—replacing our hearts of stone with hearts of flesh. Regeneration is a total change.

Louis Berkhof notes, "Regeneration consists in the implanting of the *principle* of the new spiritual life in man, in a radical change of the *governing disposition* of the soul. In principle it affects the whole man: the intellect, 1 Cor. 2:14; 15; 2 Cor. 4:6; Eph. 1:18; Col. 3:10;

—the will, Phil. 2:13; 2 Thess. 3:5; Heb. 13:21;—and the emotions, Ps. 42:1, 2; Matt. 5:4; 1 Pet. 1:8."[111]

Regeneration is the moment our new life begins. And it really is *new*. Jonathan Edwards said, "When the Holy Spirit regenerates the heart of a believer, 'there is a new inward perception or sensation of their minds, entirely different in its nature and kind, from anything that ever their minds were the subjects of before.'"[112]

To be born again is to be made new. And when that new life begins, everything changes. We move from hating God to loving Him and from loving sin to hating it. This does not mean we immediately enter a state of sinless perfection. We do no such thing. In fact, not to discourage you, but you will never even get close to reaching a state of sinless perfection in this life.

Sproul notes, "[R]ebirth is merely the beginning point of this process that goes on until we're glorified in heaven. The struggle continues from the day of rebirth until that day in heaven when we reach the fullness of maturity in Christ."[113] Welcome to the fight!

EPHESIANS 2:1-3

Paul characterizes for us what the unregenerate heart looks like in Ephesians 2:1-3 when he writes,

> [2:1]And you were dead in the trespasses and sins [2]in which you once walked, following the course of this

---

[111] Louis Berkhof, *Manual of Christian Doctrine* (Grand Rapids: Eerdmans, 1933), 236. He also notes, "[Regeneration] is an Instantaneous Change. The assertion that regeneration is an instantaneous change implies two things: (1) that it is not a work that is gradually prepared in the soul; there is no intermediate stage between life and death; and (2) that it is not a gradual process like sanctification, but is completed in a moment of time," 236-237.

[112] Kidd, *America's Religious History*, 37.

[113] Sproul, R. C. Sproul, *What Does It Mean to Be Born Again?*, Vol. 6, The Crucial Questions Series (Lake Mary, FL: Reformation Trust, 2010), 27–28.

> world, following the prince of the power of the air, the spirit that is now at work in the sons of disobedience— ³among whom we all once lived in the passions of our flesh, carrying out the desires of the body and the mind, and were by nature children of wrath, like the rest of mankind.

Let's walk through six characteristics of the unregenerate heart so that we can consider the glorious change wrought by regeneration.

1. *Dead*

This does not mean that the heart doesn't feel, or will, or act, or desire. Of course, it does. It does all those things. But the unregenerate heart does not love, will for, act in obedience to, or desire God. Rather, it loves sin. It is egocentric rather than God-centric.

2. *Walks in sin*

Paul doesn't just say that the unbeliever is dead in sin but that he *walks* in it. The unregenerate heart is one that delights in sin, which is doing what God says not to do and not doing what God says to do.[114]

This doesn't mean unregenerate people are as bad as they could possibly be. Some are very nice people, humanly speaking. But their hearts are dead and unsurrendered to Jesus. Whether they attend church or live an illicit lifestyle, they are in rebellion.

3. *Follows the course of this world*

The unregenerate heart walks the broad way and does so willingly. He follows the course of this world. He loves the world system. He subscribes to worldly morality. He chases the world's dreams. He measures himself by the world's standards of success. Since he loves the world, the love of the Father is not in him (see 1 John 2:15-17).

---

[114] The Baptist Catechism answer 17 notes, "Sin is any want of conformity unto, or transgression of, the law of God." (1 Jn 3:4)

4. *Influenced by the Evil One*

Satan is the father of lies and the epitome of rebellion against God. Those who are not born again are Satan's followers in terms of their rebellion, whether they openly acknowledge that or not. You're either a child of Christ or a child of Satan. There is no in-between.

5. *Enslaved to sinful passions*

Paul is discussing both Jews and Gentiles here. Jews trying to live an outwardly religious life and Gentiles living in open paganism were both enslaved to their sinful passions.

Every unregenerate person has a heart enslaved by sin. But it is not a victim sort of enslavement. It's a cooperating one. Men and women love the darkness more than the light. I might add here that the unbelief of the unregenerate is willful unbelief. Unbelief is not a condition. It is sin. It is a heinous and wicked sin to willfully reject Christ.

This brings us to an overarching question: Why do people sin? Because they want to. R.C. Sproul writes, "The unregenerate are under the influence of the enemy and seek fulfillment of the lusts of the flesh and the desires of the body and the mind." Perhaps you think, "Well, yes, I know some 'bad' people like that." But Sproul rightly continues, "This is not merely a description of the lifestyles of hardened criminals or convinced hedonists. This is the way everyone lives, without exception. The whole world normally and naturally lives by this fallen course."[115]

That's the nature of the unregenerate heart, according to Scripture. The lost soul is entangled with the world, the flesh, and the devil. And though he may be sorry about certain circumstances or consequences he has found himself in, he does not ultimately wish to be freed from the tyranny of sin. He loves himself too much.[116]

---

[115] Sproul, *What Does It Mean to Be Born Again?*, 30–31.
[116] Though, ironically, he really loves himself too little, for if the sinner loved God, he would *rightly* love himself and not seek to destroy himself through the evils of sin.

6. *By nature, children of wrath*

Inherently, due to Adam's sin (Rom. 5:12ff), and our own willful rebellion, the unregenerate person is a child of wrath. As Lloyd-Jones rightly put it, "All people are not the children of God. Something has to happen to us first. The good news of salvation is not that we are all, always and already, the children of God; the good news is that we can become the children of God."[117]

All unregenerate persons are children of wrath and any who die in that state will suffer God's wrath eternally in hell. That's not a popular truth, but it is the most important warning a person can hear.

EPHESIANS 2:4-5

If we were to stop at Ephesians 2:3, we might feel hopeless, but Paul continues on with a glorious phrase—"but God!" Verses 4 and 5 say, "*But God*, being rich in mercy, because of the great love with which he loved us, even when we were dead in our trespasses, made us alive together with Christ—by grace you have been saved" (emphasis added).

Ephesians 2:4-5 shows us how being made alive (i.e., being born again) produces a total change. And since we found six characteristics for an unregenerate man, we will now lay out six characteristics for the born-again man. In every way depravity has touched the human condition, regeneration counteracts.

As Dr. Sinclair Ferguson writes, "Regeneration reverses... depravity, and is universal in the sense that, while the regenerate individual is not yet as holy as he or she might be, there is no part of life which remains uninfluenced by this renewing and cleansing work."[118]

Or consider the illustration Dan Phillips uses in his book, *The World Tilting Gospel*: "Without regeneration, God would just be

---

[117] Lloyd-Jones, *Born of God*, 224.
[118] Ferguson, *The Holy Spirit*, 122-123.

hosing off the pig and watching it head right back for the muck. With regeneration, the pig is no longer a pig. God does not merely make us clean. He makes us new."[119]

What does this "new" look like? Here are six truths to consider. The person born again moves:

1. *From death to life*

Our affections change at regeneration. We go from loving sin to hating it. From hating Christ to loving Him. From being dead in sin to being made alive in Christ. And as aside, *when* did God "make us alive," according to Ephesians 2:4? *When* we were dead. Paul highlights God's sovereignty in regeneration.

2. *From walking in sin to walking in righteousness*

Remember 1 John 2:29, "Everyone who practices righteousness has been born of him." Again, this doesn't mean we are perfect. It does mean there is an evident change. Our affections are changed, and as a result, so are our actions because of our regeneration.

3. *From following the world to following Christ*

Believers leave the broad road and enter the narrow gate—the regenerate turn (repent) from sin and the world, placing their faith in Christ. And because of our regeneration, we treasure Christ. We desire to follow Him. We repent of sin. We seek to obey Him. Being born has quite an effect on people. So does being born again.

4. *From following the Evil One to rejecting him*

No longer do we follow the prince of the power of the air (Satan). We are not rebels anymore like him. Those born again actively seek to reject Satan's ways, (Eph. 6:10-20).

---

[119] Dan Phillips, *The World Tilting Gospel* (Grand Rapids: Kregel, 2011), 171.

5. *From being slaves of sin to slaves of Christ*

1 Peter 2:16 says, "Live as people who are free, not using your freedom as a cover-up for evil, but living as servants of God." The word for "servants" here is the Greek word for "slave." In regeneration, our chains are gone. We are free from the enslavement of sin, but we now joyfully serve a new master, Christ, our King (1 Thess.4:1-5).

Unbelievers may live outwardly moral lives, but they do not have the ability to choose righteousness for Christ's sake. As believers, we are enabled by God to choose righteousness. Sinful passions still like to creep up because we are still living in this world. So, it's not that we never sin. But what we have in the new birth is freedom not to sin. Sin still influences us, but it is no longer our master.

Here is the key: *The Christian actually desires to live a life of faith in Christ.* He no longer *wants* to sin. Instead, he longs to please his King in every action, motivation, and desire.

This means he or she now fights against and seeks to mortify (cf. Rom. 8:13) any unholy desire. This ranges from desires like *same sex attraction* to desires to snap at your children when they get on your nerves. The Christian does not say, "I was born that way," as an excuse for any sinful actions, motivations, or desires because he or she has now been reborn in Christ. The believer has been set free from sin and is now a slave of Christ.

Above, I explained that the unbeliever is enslaved to sin, but it's an enjoyable enslavement. That means he sins because he wants to. In the new birth, this is completely flipped. The Christian is a new creation in the sense that he or she actually *wants* Christ. Believers desire to do the will of their new master, King Jesus.

I can't tell you how many people I run into that say, "Oh I *know* I should be in church more or read my Bible more or pray more or live for Jesus more" or whatever. Being born again moves from just "knowing" what is right and wrong to actually *desiring* to live for Christ.

6. *From a child of wrath to a child of grace*

Through God's sovereign grace alone, sinners move from a state of wrath into a state of grace. As my pastor friend, Jonathan Murdock, always reminds me, we are "King's kids." Christians now enjoy the gracious work of God in our souls for the remainder of our lives. We are assured that all God is doing in our lives is for our good and His glory (cf. Rom. 8:28).

The totality of regeneration manifests itself in these six realities above. This is why Jesus uses language like "birth." Regeneration is such a total change that it is likened to the first birth. As R.C. Sproul stated, "We cannot have saving faith unless the Holy Spirit has changed the disposition of our souls. Therefore, only the regenerate have faith. All the regenerate are changed. We cannot have the Holy Spirit changing the disposition of our hearts and bringing us to faith but then leaving us hanging there with no change in our lives."[120]

God changes sinners. Amen. What hope we have in the gracious power of God in the gospel. By grace, the Holy Spirit makes us alive and, as a result of our being alive, we now grow. That growth in spiritual maturity is called *sanctification*. Regeneration always results in sanctification.

People can indeed be saved on their death bed. That does happen—though not very often. And not nearly as often as some people may expect or hope for. William Guthrie wrote, "The Bible, which ranges over a period of four thousand years, records but one instance of a death-bed conversion (the penitent thief) – one that none may despair, and but one that none may presume."[121]

The usual course of the Christian life is that a person is born again and then undergoes years of sanctification as they grow in Christ. Some, who claim to have accepted Christ, never grow. That is not a problem of spiritual immaturity. The problem is that they were never truly regenerated. Living things grow!

---

[120] R.C. Sproul, *Romans* (Wheaton: Crossway, 2009), 183-184.
[121] Accessed: https://gracequotes.org/author-quote/william-guthrie.

THE NEW BIRTH IN THE OLD TESTAMENT

I want to go back to something Jesus said and show how I think He again emphasizes this total change. Consider the dialogue in John 3:9-10. "Nicodemus said to him, 'How can these things be?' Jesus answered him, 'Are you the teacher of Israel and yet you do not understand these things?'"

Now, how would Nicodemus know these things about regeneration? See, some people try to say that Jesus is talking about the ordinance of Christian baptism in John 3:5 when He says, "unless one is born of water." But how would Nicodemus know anything about *Christian* baptism? He wasn't a Christian. He was "the teacher of Israel."

Jesus is not talking about baptism in John 3:5. He's talking about something Nicodemus should have already understood. In fact, Old Testament saints were just as regenerate as New Testament Christians. All believers of all time believe as a result of their being born again.

So, naturally, we turn to the Old Testament. Something Nicodemus should have been familiar with. The key is in Ezekiel 36:25-27, where God says,

> [25] I will sprinkle clean water on you, and you shall be clean from all your uncleannesses, and from all your idols I will cleanse you. [26] And I will give you a new heart, and a new spirit I will put within you. And I will remove the heart of stone from your flesh and give you a heart of flesh. [27] And I will put my Spirit within you, and cause you to walk in my statutes and be careful to obey my rules.

First, notice all the "I wills" in those verses. This again reinforces the teaching that God causes regeneration, not man. God removes our dead hearts of stone and replaces them with living hearts of flesh. Note all that is taking place in this regenerating work of God:

1. *He cleanses us*

This reminds me of Titus 3:5. "[H]e saved us, not because of works done by us in righteousness, but according to his own mercy, by the washing of regeneration and renewal of the Holy Spirit."

We see that Jesus uses "water" in John 3 in order to connect His teaching with the Old Testament idea of God's purifying His people's hearts with "clean water." Water on the skin does nothing for the deadness of the heart. What the sinner needs is the cleansing of the Holy Spirit in regeneration.

Baptism doesn't cause regeneration. Rather, regeneration is likened to a washing of our hearts.

2. *He gives us a new heart, taking away the heart of stone*

In regeneration, the Holy Spirit indwells us, and our heart moves from death to life. This is similar to what we saw above in Ephesians.

When Jacob came upon the shepherds in the land of his mother's people, they could not water the flocks until the large stone had been removed. The order was, "the stone is rolled from the mouth of the well; *then* we water the sheep," (Gen. 29:8).[122] Similarly, living water never flows freely inside a person until their stony heart is first removed. In regeneration, God gives us a new heart by first removing the cold heart of rebellion against Him.

3. *The Spirit causes us to walk in God's ways*

Paul says in Philippians 2:13, "[I]t is God who works in you, both to will and to work for his good pleasure." The point here is that God's people desire to follow God's ways. To love God is to desire to obey His Word, trusting His provision in Christ. This is because the Spirit Himself is causing us to walk in newness of life.

This should have been a familiar passage for Nicodemus, from Ezekiel 36. And this is not the only text in the Old Testament relevant to regeneration. Nicodemus should have known passages

---

[122] Emphasis mine.

like Deuteronomy 30:6 which says, "And the LORD your God will circumcise your heart and the heart of your offspring, so that you will love the LORD your God with all your heart and with all your soul, that you may live." God circumcising the heart is regeneration.

Nicodemus should have known Jeremiah 31:33 which says, "For this is the covenant that I will make with the house of Israel after those days, declares the LORD: I will put my law within them, and I will write it on their hearts. And I will be their God, and they shall be my people." God putting His laws within His people so that they obey Him from the heart is His supernatural work of regeneration.

Again, this is something even the saints of the Old Testament experienced. As Phillip Griffiths writes, "The Spirit has always been at work, regenerating the elect and uniting them to Christ…[A]ll men are either of the flesh or of the spirit, and all Old Testament believers were of the spirit, having been made alive by the Holy Spirit (Rom. 8:6)."[123]

Thus, Nicodemus should have understood his need for a new heart. He should have taught on all of these Old Testament passages about God's work to remove the heart of stone and replace it with a heart of flesh. Instead, he was too busy being concerned only about outward behavior.

It's not that outward behavior doesn't matter. It's that an inward change must take place to truly bring about a holy life. This is what I mean when I say regeneration produces a total change in a person.

Samuel Renihan beautifully describes the total change of regeneration when he writes,

> Regeneration is the birth of a child of God, the birth of the offspring of Christ, the birth of an inheritor of the new creation (John 3:3). It is the transfer of a member of the kingdom of darkness to the kingdom of the beloved Son (Colossians 1:12). It is a movement from Adam to Christ (1 Corinthians 15:48). It is an escape

---

[123] Phillip D.R. Griffiths, *Covenant Theology: A Reformed Baptist Perspective* (Eugene, OR: Wipf & Stock, 2016), 167.

from the Covenant of Works and an implantation in the Covenant of Grace. It is the beginning of experiential blessings in the covenant. It is the application of new creation life to a sinner, an initial deposit of glory and holiness that will grow from that point onward.[124]

A MYSTERIOUS CHANGE

Though regeneration is such a total and colossal change, it is also a mysterious change. This is what Jesus describes in John 3:8, "The wind blows where it wishes, and you hear its sound, but you do not know where it comes from or where it goes. So it is with everyone who is born of the Spirit."

When this occurs, you don't automatically say, "Oh look! I'm being regenerated now!" Rather, as John L. Dagg writes, "The mode in which the Holy Spirit effects this change is beyond our investigation. All God's ways are unsearchable, and we might as well attempt to explain how he created the world, as how he new-creates the soul."[125] Dagg goes on to say, "[I]n his own time and manner, God, the Holy Spirit, makes the word effectual in producing a new affection in the soul: and, when the first movement of love to God exists, the first throb of spiritual life commences."[126]

We know a change has taken place. But it can take time to realize all the implications of that transformation. We do not see where the wind comes from. Louis Berkhof notes, "Regeneration is a secret and inscrutable work of God that is never *directly* perceived by man, but can be perceived *only in its effects.*"[127]

How do you know you're born again? Because you love Christ. You believe on Christ. You walk with Christ. You have been transformed by the power of God in the gospel. You obey from

---

[124] Samuel Renihan, *The Mystery of Christ: His Covenant & His Kingdom* (Cape Coral, FL: Founders, 2019), 165.
[125] John L. Dagg, *Manual of Theology*, https://founders.org/library/manual-of-theology-john-dagg/dagg-bk-7-chapter-iii/
[126] Dagg, *Manual of Theology*.
[127] Berkhof, *Manual of Christian Doctrine*, 237. (emphasis original)

the heart (cf. Rom. 6:17). His will becomes more important than your own. You seek to walk the ancient paths He has set before you (cf. Jer. 6:16).

I wonder though, can you mess this up? I mean, sure, God changes you, but can you do anything to destroy that? Can you take your heart which is now alive and somehow make it spiritually dead again? Can those born again go back to being unborn? Adam messed up in the Garden and was banished from Eden. Is there a way for a true believer to fall from grace? We'll answer those questions as we now turn to consider the longevity of regeneration.

8
LASTING CHANGE: THE LONGEVITY OF REGENERATION

I love Christmas. If my wife would let me, we would put the Christmas tree up in June (Narrator: She does not let him). But this doesn't stop me from talking her into putting it up by the end of October! I have some Christmas ornaments from my childhood that I love putting on the tree because this reminds me of happy times growing up. One ornament I take particular care with is a glass Mickey Mouse that my late paternal grandmother bought me for my third Christmas in 1988.

Each year I carefully unwrap it and place it a bit higher on the tree, out of reach of tiny hands. When I take it down, I am careful to package it correctly in order to preserve it for the following year. But, eventually, no matter how much care I put into protecting this little keepsake, one day it's going to break, or be lost, or be passed down to a descendant who trashes it. Because nothing lasts forever, right?

When it comes to material possessions, the maxim indeed holds. Nothing lasts forever. However, it's not entirely true that *nothing* lasts forever. And that brings us to this chapter's subject: We've discussed the necessity, sovereignty, and totality of regeneration. Now we will examine its *longevity*. You see, the Bible teaches us that being born again *does* last forever. It cannot be undone. Regeneration is a permanent change.

BORN FROM ABOVE

As we have repeatedly noted, Jesus says in John 3:3, "You must be born again." Another translation for the word "again" is "from above." The same word is used in Matthew 27:51 for the veil being torn from "top" to bottom.

The Lexham Theological Wordbook notes, "In John 3, Jesus speaks with Nicodemus about being 'born (*gennaō*) again (ἄνωθεν, *anōthen*).' The word *anōthen* can mean either 'from above' or 'from the beginning, again,' so the whole phrase may mean either 'born from above' or 'born again.'"[128]

Physical birth is one thing. But to see the Kingdom, you must have a new birth from above. This highlights again what we examined regarding the sovereignty of God in regeneration in the previous chapters. The new birth is from above. It is God's doing.

That fact is important for our discussion in this chapter. How permanent is this new birth? If the new birth is from below and caused by man, what's to say we can't "uncause" it? Jesus says no one can snatch us out of His hands, but what if we just want to walk out? Can we become unborn again?

Those who hold to synergism *consistently* believe regeneration can be lost.[129] My argument is that since God alone causes the new birth, it is a permanent change in a person's life. So, just like a person who is born can never be "unborn" so too can a person who is born again never be unborn again. This being born again is from above and cannot be undone by someone from below. Regeneration is a permanent act of God.

---

[128] William A. Simmons, "Regeneration," ed. Douglas Mangum et al., *Lexham Theological Wordbook*, Lexham Bible Reference Series (Bellingham, WA: Lexham, 2014).
[129] Some Lutherans also believe regeneration can be lost, thought they claim to be monergists.

REGENERATION AND CONVERSION

"Regeneration…is a change of heart that leads to true repentance and faith."[130] Hence, the new birth produces immediate faith and repentance whereby the soul chooses to turn from sin and savingly apprehend Christ Jesus. Through this grace alone, by faith alone, the sinner is justified before God, being imputed (credited) with the righteousness of Christ forever.

In his systematic theology, James Boyce, an early Southern Baptist, wrote, "Regeneration is the work of God, changing the heart of man by His sovereign will, while conversion is the act of man turning towards God with the new inclination thus given to his heart."[131] Dr. James Renihan shows us how these two realities go together when he notes, "Dead sinners do not will themselves to regeneration and conversion, but those in whom the Spirit has worked by the word *freely will* to come to Christ *by his grace.*"[132]

So these two truths, regeneration and conversion, go hand in hand. Regeneration results in an individual's "voluntary obedience to the gospel" – that is, faith and repentance that endures to the end.[133] A Christian *can* never and *will* never unchoose Christ because his choice of Jesus is rooted in God's eternal choice of him (Eph. 1:3-14). This is proven by the gospel taking root in one's soul.[134]

---

[130] Thomas J. Nettles with Steve Weaver, *Teaching Truth, Training Hearts: The Study of Catechisms in Baptist Life* (Cape Coral, FL: Founders Ministries, 2017), 162.

[131] James P. Boyce, *Abstract of Systematic Theology* (Cape Coral, FL: Founders, 2006), 374.

[132] James M. Renihan, *To the Judicious and Impartial Reader: An Exposition of the 1689 London Baptist Confession of Faith*, Baptist Symbolics Vol. 2 (Cape Coral, FL: Founders, 2022), 262. (emphasis original)

[133] The New Hampshire Confession of Faith (1833). Article VII. The whole article reads, "We believe that, in order to be saved, sinners must be regenerated, or born again; that regeneration consists in giving a holy disposition to the mind; that it is effected in a manner above our comprehension by the power of the Holy Spirit, in connection with divine truth, so as to secure our voluntary obedience to the gospel; and that its proper evidence appears in the holy fruits of repentance, and faith, and newness of life."

[134] As Paul says in 1 Thess.1:4-5a, "For we know, brothers loved by God, that he has chosen you, because our gospel came to you not only in word, but also in power and in the Holy Spirit and with full conviction."

Consider 1 Peter 1:23. "[Y]ou have been born again, not of perishable seed but of *imperishable*, through the living and abiding word of God" (emphasis mine). The only way any person is born again is by the power of God through the proclamation of the gospel.[135] Peter maintains that this is an imperishable seed. The gospel is living and abiding. We can expect that the change the gospel brings is permanent to the soul.

In Isaiah 43:13, God says, "Also henceforth I am he; there is none who can deliver from my hand; I work, and who can turn it back?" There, the Lord speaks of sovereignly delivering His people. But the principle remains for the New Testament. When God works, who can turn it back?

Thus, since regeneration is God's doing, it cannot be turned back. As the hymn writer said, "I have decided to follow Jesus. No turning back. No turning back." Regeneration, God's sovereign work, produces a decision that will never be undone, not merely a single act of faith, but a life of faith and repentance.

AN ILLUSTRATION

In Ephesians 2:8-9, Paul writes, "For by grace you have been saved through faith. And this is not your own doing; it is the gift of God, not a result of works, so that no one may boast."

Now consider this line of reasoning for a moment. Pretend there were two genuine Christians, and one of them became unregenerate. How did he become unsaved? Well, some would say because he sinned or walked away from the faith.

This would mean, however, that the other Christian has something to boast about. If one Christian could become unregenerate by his choice to walk away or reject God's preserving grace, then all the Christians who remain saved to the end ultimately remain so by their own power. This means they could boast that they kept themselves in the faith – with God's help, of course.

---

[135] The concept of how infants go to heaven when they die in infancy is beyond the scope of this book.

Yet, this is absolutely antithetical to grace. Grace began our journey, and grace will lead us home. Regeneration is such a radical renewal that it is a permanent change. All who have truly been born again will make it to the end and give God alone all the glory for finishing the race. Why do I say "truly" born again? Because false believers are a reality.

Do you remember John 2:23-25? John uses the same word for "believe" there that he uses elsewhere about people savingly believing on Christ. But what's different at the end of John 2 is that He shows us these people were not true believers.

Therefore, people can and do make outward professions of faith without truly being born again. Outward professions alone do not endure to the end.[136] Christ is only enduringly endeared to those who have been born from above. Only those who've been born from above are true believers and it is only those who persevere to the end. To say one is born again and to truly be born again aren't always the same thing.

PRESERVATION AND PERSEVERANCE

We need to be reminded of two similar-sounding words when we are talking about believers making it to the end. The first is *preservation*.

The First London Baptist Confession of Faith (1644) states,

> Those that have this precious faith wrought in them by the Spirit, can never finally nor totally fall away; and though many storms and floods do arise and beat against them, yet they shall never be able to take them off that foundation and rock which by faith they are fastened upon, but shall be kept by the power of God to salvation, where they shall enjoy their purchased possession, they being formerly engraven upon the palms of God's hands. (Paragraph XXIII)

The Apostle Peter says that Christians, "by God's power are being

---

[136] Matt. 7:21-23.

guarded through faith for a salvation ready to be revealed in the last time" (1 Pet. 1:5). In other words, the Lord preserves believers in the faith so that they "can never finally or totally fall away."

Some people think of this as God preserving Christians by writing their names down and putting those names in a filing cabinet and locking it securely. But that's not the biblical idea of preservation. Instead, preservation is like God planting a seed and that seed growing over time and God protecting that plant so that it will never be plucked up. He continues to nurture that plant and provide that plant with what it needs to make it to the end. He brings the sunlight and, when necessary, the rain to ensure the plant produces fruit.

And this leads to the second P-word: *perseverance*. Preservation and perseverance are not the same thing, but they are intricately connected. Perseverance flows from preservation. Perseverance does not mean that God places you in a locked filing cabinet while you continue to live like the world, but your ticket to heaven remains secured. Rather, perseverance is like the plant that continues producing fruit. God preserves us in such a way that we *persevere*.

For example, Romans 8:12-13 says, "So then, brothers, we are debtors, not to the flesh, to live according to the flesh. For if you live according to the flesh you will die, but if by the Spirit you put to death the deeds of the body, you will live." God preserves believers in such a way that they ultimately persevere in killing sin – all a product of Christ's work for His people (cf. Matt. 1:21).

True believers have been born again, and grace has changed our affections, attitudes, and actions. We have the Holy Spirit living inside of us, so now that we are alive in Christ, we grow. The Holy Spirit's indwelling us causes us to persevere in fighting sin, loving the church, cherishing the Scriptures, growing in our understanding of God, and sharing Christ with a lost and dying world. All true believers persevere in the faith.

However, the Baptist Faith and Message (2000) says, "Believers may fall into sin through neglect and temptation, whereby they grieve the Spirit, impair their graces and comforts, and bring reproach on the cause of Christ and temporal judgments on themselves; yet they shall be kept by the power of God through faith unto salvation." That's preservation—being kept by God.

One autumn, my family had the opportunity to visit Colorado. As we explored a particularly rocky slope, my 4-year-old grabbed my hand in order to keep from falling. What he didn't fully realize at the time is that it wasn't his grip on me that kept him from danger. It was my grip on him! Praise God that He holds us even when we stumble (Jude 1:24-25).

The problem is that sometimes true believers do sin and sometimes egregiously. And sometimes, our comforts are removed. Sometimes we may even doubt our salvation. Take note: It is the kindness of the Lord to remove His comfort from us when we sin so that we might be brought back to Him.

If we truly belong to Christ, we cannot remain comfortable in our sin. If you are comfortable in sin, if you just tout "once saved always saved" to live a worldly lifestyle apart from the local church and are in love with this world, and the flesh, and sin; then I have great concern for your soul. And so should you.

As John Flavel wrote, "if you live earthly and sensual lives, as others do, you must cross your new nature therein; and can those acts be pleasant unto you which are done with so much regret? . . . Earthly delights…are suitable enough to the unregenerate and sensual men in the world, but exceedingly contrary unto that Spirit by which you are renovated."[137]

It is impossible for the believer to live comfortably in sin because we have been given a brand-new heart that desires holiness and righteousness, (cf. Eph. 4:24). True believers experience God's discipline when we sin, and true conviction and a longing to be restored in grace.

Too many people claim to have had some sort of religious experience and have been told never to doubt their salvation. As a consequence, they carry on nonchalantly like the rest of the world.

---

[137] Flavel, *The Whole Works of the Reverend John Flavel*, Vol. 2, 366.

But true regeneration produces in us steadfast perseverance—even if there are times that we find ourselves in sin.

True believers cannot utterly and finally fall away from God. And they should exercise the "means of grace" to grow in holiness.[138] When they fail to do this, at times, they can fall headlong into sin.

Some true believers may walk dangerously close to turning their backs on Christ (cf. Heb. 3:12). This is a miserable state for the soul and one in which a Christian cannot long endure. It was in this state that David said, "For day and night your hand was heavy upon me" (Ps. 33:4). This is not a place a true believer can live for very long. Thus, every professing believer ought to be thoroughly attentive to his or her spiritual state.[139]

The way we remain diligent about the care of our souls is to remember that the Lord uses various biblical means to persevere us in the faith:

- The local church.
- True fellowship with other believers.
- The ordinances.
- The preaching of the Word.
- Prayer.
- Reading the Bible, etc.

Without these, true believers can fall into grave error.

However, the longevity of regeneration means the truly regenerate will never ultimately *fall away*. And anyone who does fall away was never born again to begin with. That's why John says in 1 John 2:19, "They went out from us, but they were not of us; for if they had been of us, they would have continued with us. But they went out, that it might become plain that they all are not of us."

---

[138] "The phrase [means of grace] is intended to indicate those institutions which God has ordained to be the ordinary channels of grace, i.e., of the supernatural influences of the Holy Spirit, to the souls of men." Charles Hodge, *Systematic Theology*, Vol. 3 (Oak Harbor, WA: Logos Research Systems, Inc., 1997), 466.

[139] Owen, *The Works of John Owen*, Vol. 6, 341.

Lloyd-Jones says, "The regenerate abide. They may backslide, they may fall into sin, they may fail, but they abide, because the life is there…[O]thers may appear to be fully Christian but if there is no life they will not abide. Life shows itself, it gives proof of its existence."[140]

The character of the regenerate heart will not ultimately abandon the faith or plunge into grievous sin and just stay there unmoved. A truly changed heart does not desire to walk as close to apostasy as possible. Instead, the believing heart desires to walk evermore closely with Christ.

THE PERSEVERING GOSPEL

I want to return to a verse I mentioned earlier. 1 Peter 1:23 says, "since you have been born again, not of perishable seed but of imperishable, through the living and abiding word of God." This gospel by which we have been born again is also the living and abiding gospel that sustains us. The gospel doesn't merely begin our relationship with Christ. It maintains and nourishes our relationship.

We need a constant reminder that our relationship with God is not founded upon our merit or behavior. It's not based upon us at all! It's based upon the finished work of Jesus Christ. My sins were imputed to Christ on the cross. He bore them all. And by grace through faith, His righteousness is credited to me. On my good days and bad days, I must constantly refresh myself in this glorious reality.

The gospel got us into this, and the gospel will sustain us and bring us all the way home. What this good news does is free us to obey the Lord with joy. And when we falter, we have an advocate with the Father, Jesus Christ, the Righteous (1 John 2:1).

ETERNAL SECURITY

Eternal security has too often been used as a license for continual rebellion against God. Shame on anyone who would use God's

---

[140] Lloyd-Jones, *God the Holy Spirit*, 94.

grace as an excuse for sin![141] Unfortunately, I have known people who think that if a person says he is saved, we have no right to question that or discuss it further with him. That's simply not true or biblical.

It is the local church's responsibility to watch over one another in the Lord. Heb. 3:12-13, Matt. 18:15-18, Col. 1:28, 1 Pet. 5:8, and Gal. 6:1-2 all teach us this. This is because it really is possible for people to say they are a Christian when their heart is not born again. Therefore, God has ordained the local church to watch over its members so that this doesn't happen. This is not one subset of Christians watching over everyone else. Rather, the Bible calls upon all true believers to "exhort another every day" (Heb. 3:13).

When we have a biblical understanding of regeneration, we see that eternal security is real. Those born from above will never be *unborn* by anything below. Regeneration is permanent. Being born again is not like a favorite Christmas ornament that will one day break or fade away. Regeneration lasts forever.

We now close both this chapter and Part II of this book. So far, we have sought to understand the current evangelical predicament we find ourselves in as well as the essential nature of regeneration. We now move into the "so what" section of this book. Why does understanding regeneration rightly matter so much? What we will find is that sound theology is woven together like a beautiful coat. If you begin to tug on one thread too hard as though it doesn't matter, like the doctrine of regeneration, you may wind up finding yourself very cold in the winter!

---

[141] Paul's very argument in Rom. 6:1-2.

PART III

WHY REGENERATION MATTERS

In Part III, I'll endeavor to show why it matters that we correctly understand the doctrine of regeneration. It is certainly not my conviction that only those who have a proper view of regeneration are truly saved! George Whitefield said that he "saw regenerate souls among the Baptists, among the Presbyterians, among the Independents and among the [Anglicans]…all children of God, and yet all born again in a different way of worship."[142]

Thus, there are true believers across denominational lines—even in denominations that misunderstand some of the truths taught so far in this book. However, a correct understanding of regeneration can help keep the church and individual Christians from errors, some of them quite serious.

First, we will see that regeneration matters because the Bible is trustworthy. We begin with the idea that to deny the Bible's teaching on regeneration is to undermine the Bible itself. From there we move to the doctrine of the Holy Spirit. Regeneration matters because the

---

[142] Kidd, *America's Religious History*, 39.

Holy Spirit is God. To deny monergism is to slight the Holy Spirit's glory as though He needs man's help to do His work.

Thirdly, we move from God to the church. A proper understanding of what it means to be born again matters practically because the local church is only for those made new by the Holy Spirit. If we misunderstand regeneration, we will ultimately misunderstand the church.

Fourthly, we move deeper inside the church as we consider Baptism and the Lord's Supper. By understanding regeneration rightly, we see these ordinances as beautiful signs and symbols by which God reminds His people of the cross and blesses and strengthens His church.

Finally, we move from inside the church to outside. A right understanding of regeneration matters because authentic evangelism is essential. When we trust the Bible, and honor the Holy Spirit, we seek to be fervent and intentional in our evangelism knowing that God really does save sinners through the preaching of the gospel.

Part III seeks to connect the theological to the practical. Theology really does matter. It's not just for coffee shop conversations or seminary examinations. It matters in the trenches of ministry. It matters at the hospital bedside. It matters in the home. It matters in the church. It matters on the streets. It matters in the daily life of all who call themselves Christians.

9
BECAUSE THE BIBLE IS TRUSTWORTHY

I am not what you would call a handyman. In fact, putting my name and "handyman" in a sentence is an insult to handymen all around the world. Too often, I'm the guy who, instead of worrying about making something work the right way, just tries to make something work in whatever way. It's like I get so busy that I cut a few corners here or there in order to "fix" a problem.

What I have learned over the years, however, is that cutting corners does not ultimately save time or money in the long run. Things around the house are designed to fit together in a certain way. And it's when you operate within that design that you actually find the most practical way to make the proper repairs.

An analogy can be made with theology. Unfortunately, so many want to skip over sound doctrine in order to rush to the "practical" aspects of Christianity. The truth is, sound doctrine *is* practical. And when it is skimmed or skipped over to get to the practical, what often happens turns out to be very impractical – a misunderstanding or twisting of sound doctrine that results in false believers and unhealthy churches. To cut corners in theology damages the church.

Thus, what we want to do in Part III of this work is to flesh out why understanding regeneration rightly matters practically. The new birth is not merely a truth to be examined like a frog in a science lab. Rather, understanding it rightly matters on numerous practical levels—so many that we will not be able to cover them all in this book.

A SUMMARY

Before we tackle the first practical implication of understanding regeneration rightly, it will behoove us to do a quick summary of where we have been.

Jesus says to Nicodemus in John 3, "You must be born again." And from that, we've seen:

1. The *necessity* of regeneration

Must is a word of necessity. One cannot be a Christian apart from the impartation of new life. I'm using that synonymously with a renewed nature, a new heart, and new affections. Man is so lost in sin and in love with the darkness that his only hope is to be born again by the grace of God in the heralding of the gospel.

2. The *sovereignty* of regeneration

The necessity of regeneration leads right into the sovereignty of God in regeneration. Jesus said, "For out of the heart come evil thoughts, murder, adultery, sexual immorality, theft, false witness, slander," (Matt. 15:19). And as Keach preached, "The heart is evil and not good, until it is changed or new made; which none can do but God himself."[143]

God alone is the cause of regeneration. Remember 1 Peter 1:3. God "has caused us to be born again." The Bible's language is key here. You didn't birth yourself and you don't rebirth yourself. Paul says we are dead in our sins as unbelievers.

---
[143] Keach, *An Exposition of the Parables and Express Similitudes of Our Lord and Saviour Jesus Christ*, 121.

As John Frame says, "Death can't produce life. Only God can. So, in the new birth we are passive."[144] When Jesus says you must be born again that's an *indicative* statement, *not an imperative*. It's what must happen to us, not what we are commanded to do.

The sovereignty of regeneration means that God's sovereign grace is what brings about the new birth. God does not cooperate with sinners. There are no negotiants to be had. We bring nothing to the table. Regeneration is monergistic.

3. The *totality* of regeneration

Jonathan Dickinson preached, "Regeneration is a new spiritual and supernatural principle wrought by the Spirit of God in all the faculties of the soul, inclining and enabling unto the exercise of a life of faith in Christ and new obedience to God."[145]

Being born again is a *total* change. Jesus uses this language of birth to show us that being born again changes everything about us. You don't see regeneration as it happens, but you definitely notice its effects, (John 3:8). Our motivations, desires, actions, will, and affections all encounter the transforming, life-giving power of grace.

4. The *longevity* of regeneration

The ultimate effect is repentance from sin and faith in Christ. A life of sanctification follows this initial act of repentance and faith.[146] Though Christians are far from perfect, regeneration is a permanent change.

Believers are preserved by God and persevere in the faith. Christians fight sin and grow in holiness. Everyone born again makes it heaven.

---

[144] John M. Frame, *Salvation Belongs to the Lord: An Introduction to Systematic Theology* (Phillipsburg, NJ: P&R, 2006), 186.
[145] Roberts, *Salvation in Full Color*, 137.
[146] Of course, we have already noted that justification is by grace alone through faith alone.

SO WHAT

What we are doing in Part III of this book is answering the "So what" factor. What about all this sound doctrine? So what if we don't get this right? What difference does it make, practically speaking?

Let me start with an emphatic statement. I'm not saying if we get this wrong that we aren't Christians. In fact, I know there will be people in heaven who never fully understood this doctrine of regeneration. Some may believe, "I am born again because I did this act." And they would be wrong. But they might actually be born again. They may just be wrong on how it happened and Who did it.

Being a Christian is about trusting the finished work of Christ, trusting His perfect life, substitutionary death, and victorious resurrection. A genuine Christian is one who has been born again and embraced the gospel by grace through faith – repenting of their sins and seeking to follow Christ.

So, you might get this doctrine of regeneration wrong and still be a Christian. However, what I am arguing is important. Believing rightly about regeneration is extremely practical to our Christian life in so many ways. And true Christians care about sound doctrine enough not to remain ignorant about it. If you disagree with what I am saying about regeneration, I ask you to continue to study the Scriptures carefully and let them speak for themselves. The evidence is clear.

FOR THE BIBLE TELLS ME SO

This leads right into our first reason for getting regeneration right. Why does it matter that we get regeneration right? The first answer is because the Scriptures teach it.

Now, I know that is an obvious answer. But I want to press this issue for a moment. It really begins here. Do we trust the Scriptures or not? And if we don't trust the Scriptures, that's not where we want to be, is it?

One of the most essential things about any Christian is that he or she trusts (and obeys) what the Bible says. If we affirm the inerrancy of Scripture but do not bow to its authority or trust its sufficiency, we do not actually honor God or His Word. Jesus says, "My sheep hear my voice and I know them and they follow me" (John 10:27). True believers desire to listen to the Master's voice in the Scriptures, believe what He says therein, and obey their King.

Jesus placed a high value on Scripture because the Scriptures are the very words of God and the very source of our understanding of the truth. So, when James says in James 1:18, "Of his own will he brought us forth by the word of truth, that we should be a kind of firstfruits of his creatures," do we believe that?

By the way, it's important to mention here that just like any given verse only has one accurate interpretation, so too, when the Bible teaches us doctrine, it only gives us one meaning. The Scriptures often provide us with various *perspectives* of a doctrine, but the Bible doesn't teach one thing in one place and then give something contradictory in another place. Thus, the Bible doesn't teach, for example, both monergistic and synergistic regeneration. God's Word does not and cannot contradict itself.

So, as we've thought about the necessity, sovereignty, totality, and longevity of regeneration, the question is, will we believe what the Scriptures have to say about it? There is only one right way to understand the relationship between regeneration and faith and that is that faith is a fruit of God's work in the new birth, not the mechanism that activates being born again. We savingly believe on Christ only because of the Holy Spirit's work in regeneration.[147]

Why then might someone not believe the Scriptures' teaching on this doctrine of regeneration? I want to give you five reasons.

1. Rebellion

Here of course, is the worst problem of all the five reasons I'm going to give you. The Psalmist says in Psalm 119:155, "Salvation is far from the wicked, for they do not seek your statutes." To blatantly reject the Bible's teaching on regeneration does not bode well for one's status with the Lord.

---

[147] Frame, *Salvation Belongs to the Lord*, 186.

To rebel against God's Word is to rebel against God Himself. One characteristic of a genuine Christian is that we love God's Word. Psalm 119:97 says, "Oh how I love your law! It is my meditation all the day." We can't love the Word, we don't love the Word, unless we are born again.

The unregenerate hate God's Word. They do not want it controlling their lives. They will not submit to it. But as those who have fled to Christ in faith, we proclaim with the Psalmist: "Oh how I love your Law!"

Rebellion against the Bible's teaching on the new birth is not in the heart of a believer. John Owen said, "[L]et them pretend what they please, the true reason why any despise *the new birth* is, because they hate a *new life*. He that cannot endure to *live to God* will as little endure to hear of being *born of God.*"[148]

One reason, then, that some would reject the Bible's teaching on regeneration is because they remain in a state of sin and rebellion against God. Yes, they reject sound doctrine, but more pointedly, they are rejecting the God who gave us this doctrine.

As I said, this is the most serious of the five reasons. Not everyone who disagrees with the biblical teaching on regeneration is in this category, but some definitely are.

2. Ignorance

The second reason some reject the biblical teaching on regeneration is out of ignorance. I do not mean to use this term pejoratively. I only mean that when we become Christians, we don't have a full-orbed, robust understanding of every Christian doctrine. Truth must be learned. When we're first regenerated, we're mere babes in Christ—no shame in that.

Consider the great commission for a moment. Jesus says part of the church's responsibility toward making disciples is, "teaching them to observe all that I have commanded you" (Matt. 28:20a). Two things should be mentioned here.

---

[148] Owen, *The Works of John Owen*, Vol. 3, 216.

First, Jesus commands His followers to teach everything. Therefore, we do not get to pick and choose what to teach. We have to teach monergism because Christ taught it.

Secondly, and though it is obvious it needs to be stated, it is the church's job to *teach*. Teaching, therefore, implies that we should expect people aren't going to know everything when it comes to sound doctrine. This is particularly true of baby Christians.

It's one thing to know what the Scriptures teach and rebel against them. It is quite another not to know what they teach. A new Christian might not be able to answer all of our questions about monergism and effectual calling, citing simply, "One thing I do know, that though I was blind, now I see."[149] The church must teach. And Christians must desire to humbly learn from the Scriptures. Ignorance isn't an excuse forever.

3. Laziness

Jesus says in Matthew 18:3, "Truly, I say to you, unless you turn and become like children, you will never enter the kingdom of heaven." But He doesn't mean by that that we are to be childish or to remain as children in the faith.

The author of Hebrews says in Hebrews 5:12-14,

> For though by this time you ought to be teachers, you need someone to teach you again the basic principles of the oracles of God. You need milk, not solid food, for everyone who lives on milk is unskilled in the word of righteousness, since he is a child. But solid food is for the mature, for those who have their powers of discernment trained by constant practice to distinguish good from evil.

A baby grows from milk to baby food to solid food to steak. Believers grow in their faith and their understanding of sound doctrine. Consequently, to a new believer or a young believer, we can say that ignorance is to be expected, to a certain extent.

---
[149] John 9:25b

And perhaps we might also even say that some true Christians have a somewhat "justifiable" lack of knowledge of sound doctrine that can be attributed to poor teachers. But laziness is a common problem. And laziness in sound doctrine is *not* okay.

Some professing Christians are lazy when it comes to theology. They do not *want* to study. They do not *want* to search the Scriptures. And perhaps they are way too satisfied with where they are in their knowledge.

I remember a season in my own life when I was like that! I was probably about 21, and I thought, "Sure, there are some things I don't know, but I pretty much know the main stuff, so I'm good." Regrettably, a lot of professing Christians feel this way. I wish I could go back and rebuke that 21-year-old version of myself.

Laziness, however, actually *reveals* one's theology. It shows a low opinion of God and His precious Word. You see, it is not like the doctrine of regeneration is not in the Scriptures. It's right there. It's all over the place. And what easy access we have to the Bible, right? I mean, the last 20 years of Christianity in America have been incredible regarding the access we have to the Bible and resources online.

We have the Bible on our phones. When we are in line or waiting on the doctor or out for a walk, we can read or listen to our Bibles. I actually have a ton of resources just on my phone. There are tons of free resources online, sermons, commentaries, podcasts, notes – all at the literal touch of a button.

It is amazing how accessible sound doctrine really is to us in America. Take advantage of that! Listen to sermons on a walk. Grab a book on Kindle or order one and read it. Read more of the Scriptures. We don't want to be among those who profess trust in Christ but are lazy when it comes to studying His Word.

David says of the Scriptures in Psalm 19:10, "More to be desired are they than gold, even much fine gold; sweeter also than honey and drippings of the honeycomb." Studying the Scriptures to understand the truth about doctrine, such as regeneration, isn't just for vocational theologians or pastors. Deep, rich Bible study is for all who find God's Word more precious than gold and sweeter than honey.

4. Trust in human wisdom/philosophy

The fourth reason some reject the Bible's teaching on regeneration is because they think they are smarter than God. I see this a lot. That is, you start with a philosophical position and then, when you go to the Scriptures, you find that they don't line up with your position, so you refuse to trust the Scriptures because of your philosophical position.

For example, you start with a philosophical concept about libertarian free will, and you read the Bible through that lens. Of course, we all read the Bible with presuppositions. But the goal is to have the Scriptures shape our presuppositions rather than our presuppositions deny the plain reading of the Scriptures.

Some might say, "Well, people can't be *dead* in their trespasses and sins, as in corrupt, unwilling, and unable to do spiritual good because then God would be unfair in regenerating some and not others!" That is going to shape how they interpret the Scriptures. A lot of the plain teaching of the Bible will be dismissed simply because of a prior commitment to human wisdom or philosophy.[150]

The starting point, though, for understanding sound doctrine is not man but God. Thus, we start with the Scriptures, and we submit to them rather than trying to make the Scriptures submit to us. I have talked to people who I think are genuine believers who just can't get over this hump. But what we must do is continue to be patient, keep teaching and keep depending on the Spirit of God to use the Word.

The Word of God is powerful, isn't it? It's more potent than we give it credit for. Therefore, we keep teaching it and studying it and trusting that it will cause trust in human wisdom and philosophy to crumble.

---

[150] Or they will twist one verse, like John 20:31, to dismiss John 1:13, 3:3-8, and John 6:63.

5. *Tradition*

A fifth reason some reject the Biblical teaching on the new birth is man-made traditions. Of course, I understand some of these points can overlap. But what I mean in this point is one being so committed to a particular tradition that he or she will not see the Bible's truth.

For example, one might be so committed to the wrong idea of baptismal regeneration that he will not see the plain teaching of a verse like James 1:18. "Of his own will he brought us forth *by the word of truth*, that we should be a kind of firstfruits of his creatures" (emphasis mine).

Or someone might be so committed to the idea that faith causes regeneration that he won't listen to verses like 1 John 5:1, 1 Peter 1:3, Titus 3:5, Eph. 2:4-5, or Phil. 1:6. Traditions, whether they are formalized, like in Roman Catholicism, or from an informal belief system shared by man, can distort our ability to rightly understand the Scriptures. It's not that we should be against "traditions" per se, but that the Scriptures must stand over and above them. The Scriptures must shape our traditions, not the other way around.

ANCIENT WORDS EVER TRUE

The overarching point I hope I've made in this chapter is that the doctrine of regeneration matters practically because dismissing or denying it is ultimately rebelling against what the Scriptures say. This understanding of regeneration is practical because it is the Scripture's teaching. And don't we want our understanding of regeneration to line up with the Bible? Unequivocally, yes.

This may require a bit of wrestling with the Scriptures. It may even result in a completely different outlook on what you once thought about salvation. But this is what the Bible does to those hungry to know its truth.

As J.C. Ryle preached, "if the Bible be indeed true and our only guide to heaven, and this I trust you are all ready to allow, it surely must be the duty of every wise and thinking man to lay to heart each doctrine which it contains, and while he adds nothing to it, to be careful that he takes nothing from it."[151]

The Bible is our source for all sound doctrine. Everything we believe must be held up to the scrutiny of God's Word. Everything we believe must flow from this Book, for it is truth. It is in the truth we must stand, and it is by the truth that we are sanctified, (John 17:17). The Bible is worthy of our time and study.

If the Bible never presses you, never makes you uncomfortable, never leads you to question yourself, never challenges you, never changes your mind, actions, and heart, never humbles you, never convicts you...I'm not sure which translation you're using but switch now. Of course, the problem is not the "translation," is it? It's operator error. To follow Jesus is to follow His Word. It is to desire to understand and know and grow in sound doctrine. Rightly grasping the doctrine of regeneration is practical, first of all, because if we don't, we misunderstand a core truth of the Bible.

Yes, you can be a Christian and be confused on this doctrine. But why would you *want* to be confused or mistaken? Doesn't being a Christian make you want to know His Word rightly?

Psalm 111:2 says, "Great are the works of the LORD, studied by all who delight in them." Oh, how great a work of God is the new birth! May we continue to study to remove any unbiblical notions of this precious work from our minds.

---

[151] J. C. Ryle, *The Christian Race and Other Sermons* (London: Hodder and Stoughton, 1900), 15–16.

10
BECAUSE THE HOLY SPIRIT IS GOD

My grandfather served in the Air Force after World War II, and in 1954, he and my grandmother and my two aunts were stationed overseas in England. This is important to me for two reasons. First, in 1955, while still in England, my grandparents found out they were expecting their third child. This resulted in having my grandmother travel back to the United States so as to have the baby back home. That pregnancy was my father, who was born in September that year in Virginia.

The second reason this matters to me is because the English helped teach my grandparents to love hot tea. And growing up, I have many fond memories of drinking hot tea with Meemaw and Peepaw. It turns out, though, that the British are not only famous for hot tea but also for Hot Chocolate. But now I am not talking about the drink—I'm talking about the soul band who sang in 1975, "I believe in miracles!" And I want to begin this chapter by affirming that I, too, believe in miracles – though not the kind Hot Chocolate sang about.

The miracle I'm referring to is that of the new birth. Since we began this chapter with a British theme, consider what Dr. Martyn Lloyd-Jones, who ministered nearly three full decades at Westminster Chapel in London, preached – "Regeneration…is a miracle, it is supernatural."[152] Yes, I'm with the Doctor on this one. I, too, believe in miracles.

This understanding of regeneration causes us to stand in awe of God's work. But particularly, it helps us to rightly understand who the Holy Spirit is. This is because the Holy Spirit is the One who does the work of regeneration in the soul. Thinking wrongly about regeneration will ultimately lead to thinking wrongly about the Holy Spirit.

Our practical point in this chapter is that rightly understanding the doctrine of regeneration helps us to defend and glory in the divinity of the third person of the Trinity, the Holy Spirit. Understanding the doctrine of regeneration rightly matters because the Holy Spirit is God.

AN OVERVIEW OF THE TRINITY

Before we get to the connection between regeneration and a right understanding of the Holy Spirit, I want to briefly examine the doctrine of the Trinity as well as to defend the divinity of the Holy Spirit.

When we are talking about the Trinity, three principal affirmations need to be kept in mind.

1. There is only one God

The Shema begins, "Hear, O Israel: The LORD our God, the LORD is one" (Deut. 6:4). Christianity is a monotheistic religion, meaning we serve only one God.

---

[152] Lloyd-Jones, *God the Holy Spirit*, 85.

2. This one God eternally exists in three distinct persons

The Father is not the Son or the Spirit, the Son is not the Father or the Spirit, and the Spirit is not the Son or the Father. God eternally exists in three distinct persons. We don't want to use the term "separate" because the term "separate" would imply disunity within the Godhead.

So, Louis Berkhof notes, "[I]n God there are no three individuals alongside of, and separate from, one another, but only personal self-distinctions within the Divine essence."[153] Or, as Calvin says, "What I denominate a Person is a subsistence in the Divine essence, which is related to the others, and yet distinguished from them by an incommunicable property."[154]

I get it. Those sorts of quotes from theologians can seem rather complicated to work through. Our dilemma is that when we come to speak about God, we enter a whole new category. He is the Creator, and we are the creatures. We do the best we can in our creatureliness, determined to stay faithful to the testimony of the Scriptures.

What we are trying to communicate in our weak language about our glorious God is that He is eternally one in essence and three in Persons. He is not three "essences" and one "essence." That would be a contradiction. Rather, He is one essence and three Persons. The Persons of the Trinity are distinguishable but not separate.

3. Each person of the Trinity is truly and eternally God

The Father is God. The Son is God. The Holy Spirit is God. And they are not ranked within the Godhead. We say sometimes about Jesus that He is the "2nd person" of the Trinity but we are not ranking Him. The Father, Son, and Spirit are each truly and eternally God.

There is one God, one essence, and three co-equal, co-eternal, distinct persons. If you're having trouble wrapping your head

---

[153] Louis Berkhof, *Systematic Theology* (Grand Rapids: Eerdmans, 1938), 87.

[154] John Calvin and John Allen, *Institutes of the Christian Religion*, Vol. 1 (New-Haven; Philadelphia: Hezekiah Howe; Philip H. Nicklin, 1816), 135.

around how God could be one and three at the same time, don't fret. The doctrine of the Trinity is one of the most difficult to define—and one that needs to be accepted based on what the Word of God declares.[155]

Consider, for example, Matthew 28:19 where Jesus says we are to baptize disciples "in the name of the Father and of the Son and of the Holy Spirit." One "name" and yet three persons. One God in three co-equal, co-eternal persons.[156] Blessed Trinity.

Berkhof writes,

> It is especially when we reflect on the relation of the three persons to the divine essence that all analogies fail us and we become deeply conscious of the fact that the Trinity is a mystery far beyond our comprehension. It is the incomprehensible glory of the Godhead. Just as human nature is too rich and too full to be embodied in a single individual, and comes to its adequate expression only in humanity as a whole so the divine Being unfolds itself in its fulness only in its three fold subsistence of Father, Son, and Holy Spirit.[157]

THE HOLY SPIRIT IS GOD

Though we have briefly outlined the Trinity, I think it is still worthwhile to spend a little more space defending the divinity of the Holy Spirit. Usually, debates about the divinity of Jesus take center stage. But the Spirit's divinity and personhood are essential too.

The church has long confessed the Holy Spirit's divinity.

---

[155] Consider Augustine for example: "we do not dare to say one essence, three substances, but one essence or substance and three persons…Yet, when the question is asked, What three? human language labors altogether under great poverty of speech. The answer, however, is given, three "persons," not that it might be [completely] spoken, but that it might not be left [wholly] unspoken." Augustine of Hippo, "On the Trinity," in *St. Augustin: On the Holy Trinity, Doctrinal Treatises, Moral Treatises*, ed. Philip Schaff, trans. Arthur West Haddan, Vol. 3, A Select Library of the Nicene and Post-Nicene Fathers of the Christian Church, First Series (Buffalo: Christian Literature Company, 1887), 92.

[156] See another example in Matt. 3:16-17.

[157] Berkhof, *Systematic Theology*, 88.

Gregory of Nyssa (4th century) wrote, "We...confess that the Holy Spirit is of the same rank as the Father and the Son, so that there is no difference between them in anything, to be thought or named, that devotion can ascribe to a Divine nature."[158]

This confession is derived from the Scriptures. In fact, we see the Spirit of God in the very first chapter of the Bible. Genesis 1:1-3 says, "In the beginning, God created the heavens and the earth. The earth was without form and void, and darkness was over the face of the deep. And the Spirit of God was hovering over the face of the waters. And God said, 'Let there be light,' and there was light." In this passage, we have God the Father, God the Spirit, and God the Son (the Word) all active in creation.

In the New Testament, we see the Holy Spirit's divinity in places like Acts 5:3-4, where Peter interchanges the Holy Spirit (v.3) with God (v.4). Or in 1 Corinthians 3:16 Paul says, "Do you not know that you are God's temple and that God's Spirit dwells in you?" Christians are the temple of God because we are where the Holy Spirit dwells in a special way. Or in places like Ephesians 4:30, Paul says "Do not grieve the Holy Spirit of God..," affirming the Spirit's personality.

What I am stressing here is that the Holy Spirit is God. He is not the force. He is not merely a gift. He is not created. He is not an "it." He is eternally the 3rd Person of the Trinity, proceeding from the Father and the Son.

As Herman Bavinck writes, "The entire dogma of the Trinity, the mystery of Christianity, the heart of religion, the true and genuine communion of our souls with God – they all stand or fall with the deity of the Holy Spirit."[159] The doctrine of the Trinity is precious to us. To deny the Trinity is to place oneself outside of Christianity.

---

[158] Gregory of Nyssa, "On the Holy Spirit, against the Followers of Macedonius," in Gregory of Nyssa: Dogmatic Treatises, Etc., ed. Philip Schaff and Henry Wace, trans. William Moore, Vol. 5, *A Select Library of the Nicene and Post-Nicene Fathers of the Christian Church*, Second Series (New York: Christian Literature Company, 1893), 315–316.

[159] Bavinck, *Reformed Dogmatics*, Vol. 2, 312.

REGENERATION AND THE HOLY SPIRIT

Now it's time to connect the doctrine of the Trinity with the doctrine of the new birth that we have been studying. Bavinck writes, "The Christian church…has consistently…assumed a special divine activity in regeneration. Just as, to the extent it became more firmly persuaded of the necessity of internal grace, it confessed all the more decisively and joyfully the personality and deity of the Holy Spirit."[160]

Bavinck shows us an indispensable connection exists between our view of regeneration and our view of who the Holy Spirit is. My friend, Jeff Johnson, once noted that when Scripture speaks of sound doctrine, it speaks of it in the singular. Not sound "doctrines" but sound *doctrine*. And the point is that all doctrine is connected. To tweak something here or there inevitably affects other parts of doctrine—theology matters!

RETURN TO NICK AT NIGHT

With this in mind, let's travel back and examine John 3:8 again. "The wind blows where it wishes, and you hear its sound, but you do not know where it comes from or where it goes. So it is with everyone who is born of the Spirit."

Notice here that Jesus focuses regeneration totally upon the power of the Holy Spirit. There is a play on words there with the English word "wind" and "Spirit" because they are the same Greek word. The wind blows where it wishes, and so does the Holy Spirit. The word for "wish" can mean desire, want, or will. It's the same word in John 5:21 where Jesus says, "For as the Father raises the dead and gives them life, so also the Son gives life to whom he *will.*" The Spirit moves where He wills.

Jesus is a masterful teacher and uses a beautiful analogy in John 3:8 that brings out two points. The first is that when the wind blows, you see its effects. The second is you can't control the Spirit. Both truths go right to the heart of our practical understanding of the divinity of the Holy Spirit.

---

[160] Bavinck, *Reformed Dogmatics*, Vol. 4, 78.

Regeneration is not the result of baptism, a prayer, the Lord's Supper, or signing a card. The new birth is the result of the *will* of the Holy Spirit. You cannot tame the wind. You cannot tame the Holy Spirit. He will not be placed on a leash. He is not the gentleman with his hat in his hands waiting on your permission.

Let me put it to you like this:

- The Father does not need your help in choosing to save you.
- The Son does not need your help in dying on the cross for your sins and rising again.
- Why, then, would the Holy Spirit need your help in your being born again?

To misunderstand the doctrine of regeneration is to practically chip away at the doctrine of the Trinity. Salvation is a Trinitarian work—all three persons within the Godhead work in perfect harmony. And our salvation is not effected until applied to us in time by the 3rd person of the Trinity, the Holy Spirit.[161]

Ephesians 1:3 says that believers are blessed with every spiritual blessing. The soteriological blessing of regeneration and the blessings of justification, adoption, sanctification, and glorification that believers enjoy in time are the fruits of eternity past when God the Father elected particular persons and gave them to the Son. The Son agreed to be their Surety and in history, lived, died, was buried, and rose again for them. Finally, the Holy Spirit joyfully completed this covenant agreement in His approval to apply Christ's redemption to these undeserving sinners, which the Father chose before the creation of the world (Eph. 1:4). Therefore, misunderstanding the doctrine of regeneration has a direct consequence to our understanding of the Trinity.

I am *not* saying that someone who thinks regeneration is a work of God and man together is out and out denying the Trinity. I am saying that if you think regeneration is a work of God and a work of man together, you are being inconsistent, at best, in your understanding of the Trinity.

---

[161] John Flavel, *The Whole Works of the Reverend John Flavel*, Vol 2, 20.

To say the Holy Spirit needs our help in regeneration besmirches His glory. May it never be so. The wind blows where it wishes. The Spirit moves as He wills. He is sovereign. He is holy. He is in control. He is glorious. He deserves our worship.

Jonathan Edwards helpfully writes that, "Those who are in a state of salvation are to attribute it to sovereign grace alone, and to give all the praise to him, who maketh them differ from others."[162] He goes on to write how we ought to exalt God the Father and God the Son. But he does not forget the Holy Spirit! Edwards reminds Christians that they ought to also, "[E]xalt God the Holy [Spirit], who of sovereign grace has called them out of darkness into marvellous [sic] light; who has by his own immediate and free operation…opened their eyes to discover the glory of God, and the wonderful riches of God in Jesus Christ…and made them new creatures."[163]

THE HOLY SPIRIT AND MEANS

The Holy Spirit operates in conjunction with the preaching of the Word in order to bring about His sovereign regenerating work. This does not mean that the Scriptures are effective in themselves to bring a person from death to life but are "efficacious in leading to faith and conversion only by an accompanying operation of the Holy Spirit in the hearts of sinners."[164]

It's not the Word by itself that does the work but the Holy Spirit who sovereignly uses the Word to apply redemption to the sinner's whole life. One beautiful illustration we have of this comes from the Old Testament in Ezekiel 37. Set down this book for a moment and read Ezekiel 37:1-14. As you do so, I want you to take note of the word *Spirit*, the word *Breath*, and the word *winds*. These are the same Hebrew word, *"ruach."*

What we notice in this passage is the wind of the Spirit blowing as He will in accompaniment with the preaching of Ezekiel. The Spirit is willing to move over these bones to make them live.

---

[162] Edwards, *The Works of Jonathan Edwards*, Vol. 2, 854.
[163] Edwards, *Works*, Vol 2., 854.
[164] Berkhof, *Systematic Theology*, 612.

And He is sovereign and free to move over them as He wills. Yet, He chooses to operate in conjunction with Ezekiel's proclamation of God's Word. So, we see this example of these lifeless bones coming together, being brought from death to life by the power of the Holy Spirit via the heralding of the Word of Yahweh.

This is a wonderful picture of the Spirit moving as He wills. Though, He ordinarily moves in regeneration under the proclamation of the gospel.[165] Thus, we see in Scripture the willingness of the Spirit integrally connected to the means of gospel proclamation.

Every time a pastor preaches the gospel, every time a Sunday School teacher teaches the Bible, every time a co-worker shares the hope of Jesus, every time a street preacher calls those around him to look to Christ in repentance and faith, there is the potential for the Holy Spirit to move upon dry bones and bring the spiritually dead to life. It doesn't mean every time the gospel is proclaimed that the Spirit willfully moves to bring dead bones to life, but He does do this as He desires.

This highlights the sovereignty of the Spirit. The Spirit moves as He wills to bring about the effects that He desires, regardless of the sinner's initial resistance. As Daniel Scheiderer notes, "I could not stop God from showing me love and changing my heart, no matter how dead it was."[166] A biblical understanding of regeneration causes us to glory in the sovereignty, power, and divinity of the Holy Spirit – not to mention His steadfast love and grace!

THE SPIRIT AND TOTAL CHANGE

The total change brought about in the new birth is yet another connection between the Spirit's divinity and regeneration. D.A. Carson notes, "Where the Spirit works, the effects are undeniable and unmistakable."[167]

---

[165] I used the word "ordinarily" because we give special categories for infants or sometimes in cases, as the 1689 London Baptist Confession (10.3) puts it, of those "who are incapable of being outwardly called by the ministry of the Word."
[166] Daniel Scheiderer, *Still Confessing: An Exposition of the Baptist Faith and Message 2000* (Cape Coral, FL: Founders, 2020), 68.
[167] Carson, *The Gospel according to John*, 197.

Brands are very conscientious about whom they choose to promote their products. For example, there is a reason sports equipment companies are not using me to publicize their goods. Those companies do not want others looking at me and thinking that my body type is what their merchandise produces! The one promoting the product is intricately connected to the brand. It's why our current cancel culture demands that any person who says something politically incorrect can no longer represent a fashionable product. Their actions are tied to the suitableness, and perhaps even worthiness, of the brand.

Christians are a product of the work of the Holy Spirit. Regeneration results in a total change of a person—not that the person immediately becomes perfect, but that everything about him is changed. His affections are changed. The sinner previously loved self, and the world, and the flesh, and sin. Now his affections have been set upon Christ and the things of God.

The sinner's attitude is changed. His motivation for life is now to glorify God and enjoy Him forever. His actions are changed. He desires to bring his life under the full authority of Christ in every area. All of this is done by the work of the Holy Spirit.

God the Spirit is pleased to work in us and through us for His good pleasure, ever conforming us into the image of Christ through the process of sanctification (cf. Phil. 2:12-13). Just as God decided to take six days to create the world, He is pleased to take the entire course of our lives, after we have been born again, to conform us into the image of Jesus. This is the Spirit's work.

One of the most powerful passages in the New Testament about this is perhaps found in 1 Corinthians 6:9-11. There Paul says,

> [9] Or do you not know that the unrighteous will not inherit the kingdom of God? Do not be deceived: neither the sexually immoral, nor idolaters, nor adulterers, nor men who practice homosexuality, [10] nor thieves, nor the greedy, nor drunkards, nor revilers, nor swindlers will inherit the kingdom of God. [11] And such were some

of you. But you were washed, you were sanctified, you were justified in the name of the Lord Jesus Christ and *by the Spirit* of our God. (Emphasis mine)

"*How glorious a change does grace make!* It changes the vilest of men into saints and the children of God. Such were some of you, but you are not what you were."[168] This is the power of the Holy Spirit in His bringing about a total change to those who were once the vilest of offenders.

Matthew Henry continues, "The wickedness of men before conversion is no bar to their regeneration and reconciliation to God."[169] Why? Because the Holy Spirit cannot be stopped in His dispensing of sovereign grace upon whom He will! "The power of grace is greater than the power of the will of an unregenerate man. So none are too far gone for the Holy Spirit."[170]

A biblical understanding of regeneration results in a proper exultation in the work of the Holy Spirit and thankfulness for the total change He effects. What would it say about the Holy Spirit if He could not bring about these changes? What about that person who never goes to church, never shares the gospel, never reads the Bible, speaks filthy language, loves sexual immorality, but says, "Yeah, I've been born again"? What if Paul had said in 1 Corinthians 6:11, "Such *are* some of you?"

What does it say about the Holy Spirit if He cannot bring about what He wills to do within the sinner? Is He weak? Is He less than God? Is He unable to do what He pleases? Can He simply be bound or stopped dead in His tracks by sinners?

Can Lazarus say, "No, Lord, you'll not wake me!"? Can the dry bones say, "We will not assemble!"? Neither can a wretched hell-bound sinner keep the Holy Spirit from bringing about His desired effects upon the soul and course of life.

---

[168] J. C. Ryle, *The Christian Race and Other Sermons* (London: Hodder and Stoughton, 1900), 15–16.

[169] Henry, *Commentary*, 2254.

[170] Reisinger, *Today's Evangelism*, 52.

I hope you see my point. If we try to put forth an idea of a carnal Christian or a Christian who is never changed or one who is going to heaven but doesn't sincerely love the things of God, His Word, the church, evangelism, prayer, etc. then what we have done is diminish the power of the Holy Spirit. We would have to say, "There are just some people too sinful for the Holy Spirit to work."

Remember what God said in Ezekiel 36:27! "I *will* put my Spirit within you, and *cause* you to walk in my statutes and be careful to obey my rules" (emphasis mine). Praise God that none breathing are too far gone because the Holy Spirit is both gracious and sovereign. He is truly God.

Any understanding of regeneration that diminishes monergism, resulting sanctification, or the perseverance of the saints, ultimately, whether intentional or not, takes a swipe at the Holy Spirit's very "God-ness." Intellectually we may affirm the doctrine of the Trinity, but practically, we have slighted the sovereign, glorious work of the Holy Spirit. With this errant attitude, we are saying, "Aww. You really want to bring about this great change, Holy Spirit, but too bad you just can't do it." No, saints, it is frankly unacceptable and, if pressed, heretical for us to hold these views about the Holy Spirit.

If we get regeneration wrong, then at best, we are inconsistent with our understanding of the divinity of the Holy Spirit. Understanding regeneration rightly is extremely practical. It cannot be separated from the rest of sound doctrine. If we get regeneration wrong, we have misunderstood both the Scriptures and the Holy Spirit. But that's not all. In the next chapter, we'll now see what happens when the Holy Spirit begins changing hearts – local churches are formed! A right view of regeneration has a profound impact on our understanding of the local church. We turn now to exploring regenerate church membership.

11
BECAUSE THE LOCAL CHURCH IS FOR BELIEVERS

The local church has fallen on challenging times in America. Almost weekly, I encounter people in the Bible Belt who try to deemphasize the local church. "Christianity isn't about the local church!" they say. "It's about a personal relationship with Jesus!" To put it bluntly, this assessment is damning.

The New Testament doesn't know of any semblance of Christianity separated from the local church. Believers *are* the church, and they gather *with* the church on a regular basis. A local church isn't *any* gathering of Christians. It is a gathering of Christians ordered under biblically qualified male leadership, observing the ordinances of Baptism and the Lord's Supper, hearing the preached Word, and practicing biblical membership and discipline.

This idea permeates the New Testament, particularly the Epistles. We can't make sense of the Epistles without this idea of the local church. But why does the topic of the local church appear in a book about regeneration?

In *From Death to Life*, I wrote, "One of the crucial marks of what it means to be Baptist is that we believe the local church, so far as we are able to discern, is made up of regenerate members, i.e., people who have passed from death to life. Historically, Baptists have believed in regenerate church membership."[171] That's why. If we fail to understand regeneration rightly, it will inevitably have adverse consequences on our ecclesiology—our doctrine of the church.

One of the things that makes a Baptist a Baptist is that we believe in what is called *regenerate church membership*.[172] Only those who are regenerated are to be admitted as members of a local church.

To put it more pointedly, the local church is to be made up of Christians. For example, in 1 Peter 2:4-5, Peter calls the recipients of his letter, which were members of local churches, *living* stones. Therefore, our understanding of regeneration inextricably connects to our understanding of the local church.

WHAT IS A LOCAL CHURCH?

Our friend Benjamin Keach, defines a church this way,

> A church of Christ is a congregation of godly Christians, who as a stated assembly (being first baptized upon the profession of faith) do by mutual agreement and consent give themselves up to the Lord, and one to another, according to the will of God; and do ordinarily meet together in one place, for the public service and worship of God; among whom the word of God and sacraments are duly administered, according to Christ's institution.
>
> The beauty and glory of which congregation does consist in their being all converted persons, or *lively stones*; being by the Holy Spirit united to Jesus Christ, the precious corner-stone and only foundation of every Christian, as well as of every particular congregation, and of the whole *catholic church*.

---

[171] Nelson, *From Death to Life*, 191.
[172] Nathan A. Finn, "Baptist Identity As Reformational Identity," *Southeastern Theological Review Volume 8*, no. 2 (2017), 31.

> That every person before they are admitted as members, in such a church so constituted, must declare to the church (or to such with the pastor, that they shall appoint) what God has done for their souls, or their experiences of a saving work of grace upon their hearts. Moreover, the church should enquire after and take full satisfaction concerning their holy lives, or good conversations.
>
> When admitted into membership, they must solemnly enter into a covenant before the church to walk in the fellowship of that particular congregation. They must submit themselves to the care and discipline thereof and to walk faithfully with God in all his holy ordinances. They agree to be fed, have communion, and worship God there, when the church meets (if possible); and give themselves up to the watch and charge of the pastor and ministry thereof.[173]

What a robust definition! As an aside, let me say Christ is worthy of a healthy local church in every city, town, and village around the globe. Believers today must seek to recover this kind of understanding of the local church.

Keach rightly says that church members are to be Christians. One cannot be united to other believers in the local church without first being united to Christ. And one cannot be united to Christ apart from having been born again.

Keach also notes that before a person is admitted to a local church he must talk with the church or the pastors and, in their own words, describe what God has done for their souls. This is vital in affirming a person's profession before welcoming them into the church as members. This examination is not because we want to be mean, or to put someone through an inquisition. It's done to preserve the purity of the church. Though regeneration is a mysterious and

---

[173] Benjamin Keach, *The Glory of a True Church* (Conway, AR: Free Grace, 2015, 1697 Original), 21-23.

sovereign work of the Holy Spirit, as Jesus said, we can and must see the evidences of it in that person's life, (cf. John 3:8, Luke 6:43-45).

Finally, once believers join a local church they are expected to live as regenerate persons. Regeneration has affected every part of their heart. Therefore, they are expected to walk in a manner worthy of their calling (cf. Eph. 4:1). Truly, the beauty of a local church "consists in the holiness and purity of the lives and conversations of all the members."[174]

A biblical understanding of regeneration improves our comprehension of what true Christians and true churches look like. The church is not to admit every person to membership who says, "I am born again." Nor does a local church continue to walk in fellowship with those who say they believe in Christ while walking in ungodliness. Jesus did not entrust Himself to everyone who professed belief (cf. John 2:24-25, Luke 9:57-58), and neither should His Bride.

This might come across a bit surprising for some readers, so allow me to explain a little about the authority and responsibility of the church. Then, I'd like to offer some signs of regeneration the local church must look for in accepting members.

THE CHURCH'S AUTHORITY

Let's consider two weighty passages that have stirred their share of controversy over the years. In fact, a whole book could be written on one or both of these passages. Nevertheless, we must at least glance over them, albeit briefly, in this chapter.

First, consider Matthew 16:15-19. In verse 16 Jesus promises to build His church. Then He says in verse 19, "I will give you the keys of the kingdom of heaven, and whatever you bind on earth shall be bound in heaven, and whatever you loose on earth shall be loosed in heaven."

The second passage to consider is Matthew 18:15-20. This is a passage about church discipline. In verse 18, Jesus says, "Truly, I say

---

[174] Keach, *The Glory of a True Church*, 69.

to you, whatever you bind on earth shall be bound in heaven, and whatever you loose on earth shall be loosed in heaven."

What I want you to notice in these passages is Jesus's mention of the keys of the Kingdom as well as His mentioning in both passages about binding and loosing. What does this mean, and who holds these keys?

First, these texts mean that Jesus has given His local churches the authority and responsibility to carefully guard its membership. That is, Jesus has given the local church the responsibility and authority to say what is and what is not sound doctrine and to say who is and who is not a Christian.[175] Let me quickly follow that up by saying that sometimes the local church can get both of those things wrong.

Jesus doesn't give the church authority to create sound doctrine. Nor does He give the church authority or power to create a Christian or to make someone who is a Christian, not a Christian. Rather, He has simply given the local church both the responsibility and the authority to make these public declarations of truth regarding sound doctrine and genuine professors of the faith.

It is every local church's responsibility on earth – to the best of each church's ability – to proclaim what is true and not true. It is its responsibility to determine if someone has been born again, or if someone is self-deceived about their profession. Regenerate church membership means that a local church does the best it can to make sure that all the ones on her church roll are also in the Lamb's Book of Life.

Okay, but how can we possibly do this? How can we possibly know who is really a Christian and who is not? Is there some quest to embark upon whereby we may unlock the secrets to the Lamb's Book of Life and check our rolls against its infallible record?

Sorry, Mr. Baggins. There will be no unexpected journey here. The only journey we need to take is the one we've embarked upon in this book – understanding regeneration rightly. When we understand

---

[175] Jonathan Leeman, *Don't Fire Your Church Members: The Case for Congregationalism* (Nashville: B&H Academic, 2016), 77.

the doctrine of regeneration rightly, we understand that it is a total change. That a person actually moves from spiritual death to spiritual life. And that though we don't see the wind, we do see its effects. There will be signs of life in every person born again. If those signs are absent, it gives reason to doubt that their profession is genuine.

HOW TO KNOW IF YOU'RE A CHRISTIAN

The Apostle John writes in 1 John 5:13, "I write these things to you who believe in the name of the Son of God, that you may know that you have eternal life." John did not pen this epistle for fretful fruit-checking but as a way of encouragement and assurance to genuine believers so that they could rest confident in Christ and their walk with Him.

We've examined 1 John already in this book, but let's review, starting at the end of the book and working our way back toward the front. We need to do this because of an all too often scenario we typically see in churches when it comes to membership. The scenario goes something like this:

A couple visits a church a few times. One Sunday, during the invitation time, they decide to walk forward and join the church. The pastor asks them a few questions, and then they are presented before the congregation and unanimously accepted into membership on the spot.

Now, these people may be genuine believers. But, does anyone really know them yet? Again, it's possible. But it's also possible for a church to be so eager to have new members that it neglects its due diligence in evaluating a person's life before admitting them to the fold.

This exact scenario happened to me several years ago. A couple had visited the church a total of two times. They came forward at the end of the service on their second visit and wanted to join the church. I told them how excited I was to have them express such an interest, and I asked if I could meet with them that afternoon and present them before the church at a later date.

They were immediately taken aback. I mean they seemed like genuine people, but I did not really know them at all. I did not know their testimony. I did not know their views on the church. Therefore, I had some pertinent issues we needed to discuss. They agreed to meet, and I thought our meeting went well, but they never came back to the church.[176]

I share that story because I know what I'm saying is a bit countercultural regarding how things have "always been done." Doing your due diligence as a pastor of a local church may mean fewer people end up joining. But if we read the Scriptures and pay attention to the trajectory of church history, we will find that what I have presented is the truth.

It is not enough for a local church to look at the date in someone's Bible as evidence that he or she has been born again. And since Christ cares so much about the purity of His local churches, so must we.

Here is where 1 John is helpful. Let's review 1 John 5:1, 4:7, 3:9, and 2:29.

- 5:1 - Everyone who believes that Jesus is the Christ has been born of God, and everyone who loves the Father loves whoever has been born of him.
- 4:7 - Beloved, let us love one another, for love is from God, and whoever loves has been born of God and knows God.
- 3:9 - No one born of God makes a practice of sinning, for God's seed abides in him; and he cannot keep on sinning, because he has been born of God.
- 2:29 - If you know that he is righteous, you may be sure that everyone who practices righteousness has been born of him.

From these four verses, we can discern five ideas of what it looks like to be genuinely born again:

---

[176] I recommend now having a new members class to avoid this kind of confusion.

1. A regenerate person believes that Jesus is the long-promised Messiah.
2. A regenerate person, therefore, trusts God's Word.
3. A regenerate person loves Christ and His people instead of the world (1 John 2:15-17, 3:14).
4. A regenerate person fights and confesses sin (1 John 1:9).
5. A regenerate person practices righteousness.

We also need to establish that we must understand the difference between mature Christians and baby Christians. Take two baseball players, one 6 and one 16. The 16-year-old is much more advanced in how he throws, fields, and hits the ball. The 6-year-old is no less a baseball player simply because he does these things at an immature level.

With that aside, we also need to recognize that these characteristics, in some measure, are going to be present in every person who is truly born again. And I don't mean to say these are the only things evident. We might add things like a desire for reconciling with those wronged—think of Zacchaeus for example —which also includes generosity (Luke 19:10).

Or we might say a regenerate person has genuine joy in the Lord. For example, Jonathan Edwards's wife, Sarah, records her experience during the Great Awakening, citing, "So conscious was I of the joyful presence of the Holy Spirit, I could scarcely refrain from leaping with transports of joy."[177] Christians are, or should be, joyful people (cf. Phil. 4:4).

These five main points from 1 John are helpful in determining a person's spiritual standing in Christ. You know what a person who has been born the first time looks like. They will have certain *physical* characteristics. So too, the Scriptures show us what a person who has been born again looks like. They will have these certain *spiritual* characteristics.

---

[177] Edwards, *The Works of Jonathan Edwards*, Vol. 1, lxvi.

A person born again wants to join a fellow body of believers under biblically qualified male leadership and ordered rightly under the Scriptures. Regeneration does not merely affect our personal relationship with God but also moves us to now "love one another as fellow members of Christ."[178] Believers literally have a *heart* for the local church, a heart given to them by none other than the One who loves the church, sings over her in His grace, gave Himself up for her, and is working all things together for her good and His glory.

WHO CAN JOIN A CHURCH?

With this in mind, we return to the idea of regenerate church membership. The biblical description of who is born again must be every local church's standard of membership. The Bible is our final authority.

So, who can join the church? Born again sinners who are now called *saints*! That means they must believe that Jesus is the Christ, the Son of God. This means they have at least a basic understanding of the gospel. They love Christ and His people. They genuinely want to follow Jesus in baptism, and they want to plug into the local church—to love it and actively serve it.

Saints fight sin. This means they have repented of sin and turned from it. Does that mean they no longer sin? Of course not. But sin will no longer be the *pattern* of their lives.

They've left the house of the boyfriend they were living with. They have quit their drunkenness. They have forsaken self-righteousness. They have turned away from homosexuality. They now seek to live a holy life and do good works. They genuinely desire to humbly sit under the instruction of the Scriptures.

The Holy Spirit has brought about these changes in their lives through their regeneration. They have been made new. They are a new creation. They have new life.

---

[178] Anthony A. Hoekema, *Saved by Grace* (Grand Rapids; Cambridge, UK: Eerdmans, 1994), 107–108.

No, the regenerate are not perfect. They still sin. And their knowledge of the Scriptures is still ongoing. Yes, they may struggle to articulate certain doctrinal points. Yes, a regenerate 10-year-old will look different than a newly regenerate 35-year-old.

Here is a place that monergists and synergists can agree. They may disagree on the order of regeneration and faith, but they should not disagree about what regeneration produces. As I have clearly shown you, I am a monergist. But I can still work alongside synergists in the local church who agree with the total change that regeneration brings to a person's soul and subsequent outward life and behavior.[179]

I think there are two practical issues we must avoid as a local church. On the one hand, we must avoid admitting to membership every person who simply says they are a Christian. A date written in the Bible or having once recited a prayer does not necessarily indicate that a person is born again. If repeating a prayer or writing a date in the Bible were serious indications of one's regeneration, then the New Testament writers would have told us this information. It is the church's job to only admit those to the fellowship who give a credible profession – meaning it must match up with these things we've examined that *are* included in the Scriptures.

The other area we need to avoid is becoming overly cynical or harsh in this important endeavor. We must extend grace and love even as we seek to guard the truth and maintain the church's purity. Because as much as we do not want to admit unbelievers into the fold, we must be vigilant never to turn away a true believer![180] We must deal gently with infants in Christ.

Again, here is where the rubber meets the road. If we properly understand what it means to be born again, we will be greatly aided in using this to practice regenerate church membership in our churches.

---

[179] This is not to say that synergism is not a problem. I hope this book has demonstrated that it is a serious error that ought to be corrected. It is only to say that monergists and synergists can still work together.

[180] There are other things to consider, of course, like a person's willingness to agree on a church's stance on things like baptism.

And, to repeat, since Christ continues to care about the purity of His local churches, so must we.

BIBLICAL CHURCH DISCIPLINE

Understanding regeneration rightly not only aids us in determining who can join the church but also in how believers in the church are to live. This is not about playing the "salvation police." Rather, it is about obeying the Bible's command to truly "Love one another with brotherly affection" (Rom. 12:10).

Whenever church members observe one another living out of step with the reality of a changed heart, they are to confront one another in humility and love (cf. Matthew 18:15-20). Most of the time, this will result in eventual repentance, reconciliation, and correction of behavior. Sometimes, however, those who profess to be Christians will persist in sin, resulting in churches needing to "purge themselves from all pernicious members."[181]

In 1 Corinthians 5:11, Paul writes, "But now I am writing to you not to associate with anyone who bears the name of brother if he is guilty of sexual immorality or greed, or is an idolater, reviler, drunkard, or swindler—not even to eat with such a one." This is because those born again have separated from these evils. When a true believer is confronted in sin, he or she eventually repents. Those who stubbornly persist in ungodliness give no evidence of having a regenerate heart. The church, therefore, after doing her patient and loving due diligence, withdraws fellowship from these persisting in sin.

Keach writes, "The power of the keys, or to receive in and shut out of the congregation, is committed unto the church."[182] Local churches must take this responsibility and authority seriously. They must remove those unwilling to forsake their sin from the membership of the church in obedience to Christ, for the purity of the church, and in hopes that the unrepentant man or woman will turn to Christ (cf. 1 Cor. 5:5).

---

[181] Keach, *The Glory of a True Church*, 36.
[182] Keach, *The Glory of a True Church*, 35.

A healthy understanding of regeneration assists churches in this endeavor. Knowing that regeneration is the sovereign work of God that affects the totality of a person's inner spiritual life, helps local churches to hold a high standard for membership. This must be done with much grace, patience, kindness, and love. Still, it is not unreasonable for local churches to expect Christians to live like Christians.

ASSURANCE OF SALVATION

The perseverance of the saints and assurance of salvation are also threaded closely together with the local church. Understanding regeneration rightly helps us to understand what assurance should be based on and how it is achieved. And this is exactly John's argument in his first epistle.

According to 1 John, if you *say* you're a believer, but you don't love Christ's people, you don't fight sin, you don't practice righteousness, that's a problem. We have grown accustomed to thinking assurance of salvation is purely personal and subjective. But there are some objective indicators, as well.

For example, any person willfully forsaking the local church has no grounds for assurance of salvation – "We *know* that we have passed out of death into life, because we love the brothers. Whoever does not love *abides in death*" (1 John 3:14, emphasis mine).

I remember talking to a deacon at a former church once who said he knew he was saved because he felt the Holy Spirit. But John tells us to "test the spirits to see whether they are from God" (1 John 4:10). So, again, if one says they "feel" the Holy Spirit inside them, but they do not actively concern themselves with the regular meetings of their local church, it is not the Holy Spirit they feel. They are terribly and tragically deceived by their misinformed feelings.

Sometimes genuine believers struggle with their assurance of salvation. And sometimes genuine unbelievers really truly think they are saved even when they are not.[183] There is such a thing as false

---

[183] R. C. Sproul, *Can I Be Sure I'm Saved?*, Vol. 7, The Crucial Questions Series (Lake Mary, FL: Reformation Trust, 2010), 25–26.

doubt when one should have assurance and false assurance when one ought to be doubting his or her conversion.

Where, then, is the ultimate ground for assurance? The 1689 London Baptist Confession rightly says, assurance is ultimately "founded on the blood and righteousness of Christ revealed in the Gospel" (18.2). The gospel promise of justification by faith alone is our only steadfast anchor for assurance of salvation.

There may be times when genuine believers are in sin and lose their sense of assurance of their salvation, though they can never actually lose their salvation. This is actually a mercy from the Lord. You should not "feel" saved when you are in active rebellion against God, and if you do, perhaps it is because you have not genuinely been born again and are not indwelled by the Holy Spirit.

The overarching point I am making here is that a healthy understanding of regeneration has practical ramifications for understanding assurance of salvation. We must see the connection between our assurance of salvation and the local church because sometimes the church actually sees these evidences of grace in you better than you see them in yourself. And so, in seasons of doubt, the local church can encourage you in the faith to keep pressing on in Jesus.

Ultimately, all those who are regenerated persevere. There will always be pretenders in the faith who hang around for a few years or even a few decades and then fall away. This is because men "may vainly deceive themselves with false hopes and carnal presumptions of being in the favor of God and state of salvation." Those, however, who are truly born again, trusting Christ, loving His Word and His ways, "may in this life be certainly assured that they are in the state of grace, and may rejoice in the hope of the glory of God, which hope shall never make them ashamed" (18.1).

It is possible to *think* you are saved and not be saved. That's why these practical indicators are important. Does your life reflect the truths 1 John teaches us? You actually may not be able to answer that question as well as your local church can and should.

It also needs to be mentioned here that people can commit outwardly to the church while possessing an unregenerate heart. People who love "community" or feel they are honoring God with their religious efforts apart from an authentic love for Him have selfish motivations to be involved in church without being born again. This can even manifest itself in church leadership like pastors or deacons. Spiritual deception is real. The only antidote to this is to constantly strive to shape the local church in accordance with the Word of God. Keep Christ central. Make involvement in one another's lives real. All of these reasons are why healthy local churches matter.

PASTORAL WISDOM

Pastorally, I would say three things to the person who is struggling with their assurance of salvation. First, look to Christ. Trust His Promises. Trust the sufficiency of His Work. For every one look at your own life, take ten looks at Christ's!

The gospel, in one sense, can be summed up in just one word: *Christ*. There is where our anchor must lie. There is where the war must cease. There is where the eyes of faith must look. There is where the heart must rest. There is where the ears must listen. There is where the feet must follow. There is where the mind must dwell. There is where the soul must find security.

Secondly, be plugged in to the local church. Keach writes, "Brethren...the church in her public worship is the nearest resemblance of heaven".[184] Could not your soul use more heaven on earth? This you will find in a healthy local church.

Furthermore, also be committed to relationships and fellowship within the church outside its corporate gatherings. In all of this, don't schedule church around your life. Schedule your life around your local church and her members. Sit under the preaching of the Word. Commit to studying the Bible regularly with others in your church. Be in one another's homes. Regularly exhort, encourage, challenge, and love other brothers and sisters in the faith.

---

[184] Keach, *The Glory of a True Church*, 80.

Finally, to the person struggling with assurance of salvation, I would urge you to forsake known sin now and seek accountability in areas you know you struggle in. It is possible that you are struggling with assurance because you are *not* born again. Will you leave your sin? You must do so posthaste! And you must seek faithful church members to help you in areas you are failing or prone to fail.

Christianity is not a sprint but a marathon. So, keep running, looking to Christ.

CONCLUSION

Understanding regeneration rightly helps us to understand the local church. It helps us to know who should be in the church. It helps us to know how those in the church should live.

The doctrine of regeneration cannot be disconnected from other great truths of the Christian life. To err in understanding regeneration rightly is going to have significant consequences on other aspects of our theology. Those who delight in the Lord, love to study all His wondrous works (Ps. 111:2). We long to study the works of God in order to have a consistent and biblical understanding of them so as to deepen our joy in Him and bring Him glory.

We now approach our next practical chapter where we consider the beauty of the two ordinances of the local church. Baptism and the Lord's Supper do not bring about or assist in our regeneration whatsoever. Rather, they remain beautiful signs and symbols by which God blesses and strengthens His church.

12
BECAUSE THE ORDINANCES ARE BEAUTIFUL

In one sense, the Bible is a Book about three trees. First, there is the Tree of Life. This tree appears in the garden of Eden and again in Revelation 22:1. The second tree is the Tree of Knowledge of Good and Evil. This tree shows us how we lost the right to the first tree when Adam and Eve ate its forbidden fruit. Then there is the third tree.

This tree is the one they nailed our Savior to (cf. 1 Peter 2:24). This tree shows us the severity of what we lost in Genesis, but also the way back to what we will finally gain in Revelation. You would think that this third tree is kind of a big deal. And it is! So much so that God has given His churches two special ways to celebrate the cross and the salvation obtained therein. O, the wondrous cross!

In this chapter, then, we'll see a right view of regeneration helps us to properly understand the wonderful ordinances of Baptism and the Lord's Supper. The goal is not to name all of the various views on the ordinances so much as to present the biblical truth of what the ordinances are, and what they do and don't do. Rightly understanding regeneration matters because the ordinances are beautiful.

ORDINANCES OR SACRAMENTS?

Protestants have typically (and rightly) identified two biblical ordinances in the local church: Baptism and the Lord's Supper. These ordinances are seen in places like Acts 2:41, "So those who received his word were baptized, and there were added that day about three thousand souls." And 1 Corinthians 11:26, "For as often as you eat this bread and drink the cup, you proclaim the Lord's death until he comes."

Sometimes, there is lively debate on whether or not we should call these activities *ordinances* or *sacraments*. Calling them "ordinances" just means they are God-ordained. The 1689 London Baptist Confession of Faith uses the word ordinances – "Baptism and the Lord's Supper are ordinances of positive and sovereign institution, appointed by the Lord Jesus, the only lawgiver, to be continued in his church to the end of the world" (28:1).

The other word sometimes used for Baptism and the Lord's Supper is "sacrament." As Sam Waldron has written, "The term 'sacrament' comes from the Latin word *sacramentum* which simply means, something sacred."[185] So, on its surface, I don't have a problem with the word "sacrament."

However, sometimes people can use the word "sacrament" to mean that there is saving power in the ordinances. This view would say that Baptism and/or the Lord's Supper either contribute to our regeneration or prepare us for justification. If the word "sacrament" is used in that way, we adamantly need to reject it.

Sam Waldron again is helpful here. He says, "If sacrament to us is just a reverent and convenient way of speaking about the only two ordinances of Christ which make use of physical emblems, then we may find it a useful word. As long as we mean the right thing about using this word (or by not using it), then we should not argue about it."[186]

---

[185] Sam Waldron, *A Modern Exposition of the 1689 Baptist Confession of Faith. 5th Edition: Revised and Corrected* (Welwyn Garden City, UK: EP Books, 2016), 398.
[186] Waldron, *A Modern Exposition of the 1689 Baptist Confession of Faith*, 398.

I typically use the word "ordinance" so as not to be confusing, but I'm not against the use of the word "sacrament" so long as we understand what is meant by it. That's the point of this chapter. If we properly understand the doctrine of regeneration, then we understand that neither Baptism nor the Lord's Supper contributes to our regeneration.[187]

MEANS OF GRACE

The Bible clearly presents these ordinances of Baptism and the Lord's Supper as what we typically call *means of grace*. Wayne Grudem notes, "means of grace are simply means of additional blessing within the Christian life and do not add to our fitness to receive justification from God."[188]

These ordinances of Baptism and the Lord's Supper are given to the church as additional channels of blessings, if you will. They were not something God's people in the Old Testament did since they "are New Covenant positive laws."[189] Christ instituted these ordinances for His church. Therefore, the church is to participate regularly in these activities. He did not give them to add anything to our salvation, but He gave them as a comfort and encouragement to His people and to strengthen the faith of all believers.

BAPTISM AND THE SPIRIT

In the New Testament we recognize the word "baptism" is not only used to refer to physical water. For example, John the Baptist says in Mark 1:8 that Jesus is coming to "baptize you with the Holy Spirit."

---

[187] Nor do they contribute to our justification but that's really beyond the scope of this book.

[188] Grudem, *Systematic Theology*, 952.

[189] Michael Seewald, *Anticipating God's Rest: The Theology and Celebration of the Lord's Day* (Conway, AR: Free Grace, 2020), 28. Seewald defines "positive laws" this way: "If we pay close attention to God's commandments in Scripture, we see another type of law that is not intrinsic to righteousness and only serves a temporary purpose in the plan of God in this world. These laws are not natural to us. In other words, we could have no knowledge of them without God's special revelation. This type of law is often referred to in theology as positive law." 18.

Or, in 1 Corinthians 12:13, Paul says, "For in one Spirit we were all baptized into one body—Jews or Greeks, slaves or free—and all were made to drink of one Spirit."

Undoubtedly then, there is a "baptism" in the New Testament that refers to the work of the Holy Spirit (cf. Titus 3:5). The Spirit's baptism happens to us at conversion whereby we are united to Christ, including His death, burial, and resurrection. MacArthur notes, "That singular Spirit baptism occurs at conversion, when the believer is born again and placed into the sphere of the Spirit's sanctifying power and indwelling presence."[190]

Water baptism is intricately connected to this, not because it's what brings about these things, but because it is the outward and visible sign of these inward realities. R.C. Sproul writes, "even though there is a distinction between water baptism and Spirit baptism, one of the things the new covenant sign of baptism indicates is the participation of every believer in the power and anointing of the Holy Spirit. Water baptism is a sign of Spirit baptism."[191]

The Holy Spirit has done this work of immersing us (that's what the word "baptism" means) into Christ's life, death, burial, and resurrection. This is signified in the church's ordinance of water baptism which is an outward symbol of an inward reality. John MacArthur affirms, "Water baptism is…an external demonstration of what has already occurred in the heart through the regenerating power of the Holy Spirit."[192]

WATER BAPTISM

The 17th-century Baptists of England defined water baptism this way in the 1644 London Baptist Confession of Faith:

> Baptism is an ordinance of the New Testament, given by Christ, to be dispensed only upon persons

---
[190] MacArthur, *Biblical Doctrine*, 783.
[191] R. C. Sproul, *What Is Baptism?*, 1st Ed., Vol. 11, The Crucial Questions Series (Orlando: Reformation Trust, 2011), 46.
[192] MacArthur, *Biblical Doctrine*, 786.

professing faith...The way and manner of the dispensing of this ordinance the Scripture holds out to be...plunging the whole body under water: it being a sign, must answer the thing signified, which are these: first, the washing the whole soul in the blood of Christ; secondly, that interest the saints have in death, burial, and resurrection (of Christ); thirdly, together with a confirmation of our faith, that as certainly as the body is buried under water, and rises again, so certainly shall the bodies of the saints be raised by the power of Christ, in the day of the resurrection, to reign with Christ.[193]

The biblical understanding of water baptism is as a sign and symbol. In fact, one of the most important things you need to know about both ordinances is that they are visible *symbols*. They are objects to be seen, felt, and in the case of the Lord's Supper, tasted.

Samuel Renihan notes, "Baptism is...a two-way declaration. On the one hand, it is God's visible promise that all who are in His Son are new creations by virtue of their union with Christ in His death and resurrection (Rom. 6:3-5). And on the other hand, it is the individual's profession of faith in those very promises (1 Pt. 3:21-22)."[194]

1 Peter 3:21-22 says, "Baptism, which corresponds to this, now saves you, not as a removal of dirt from the body but as an appeal to God for a good conscience, through the resurrection of Jesus Christ, who has gone into heaven and is at the right hand of God, with angels, authorities, and powers having been subjected to him."

I'm going to use an illustration I adapted only slightly from my friend Jeff Johnson. Imagine a hostage situation in a foreign country. The U.S. Army is called in, and they rescue a young lady. She doesn't speak English all that well, but a reporter tries to ask her later, "Who saved you?"

---

[193] See also Chapter 29 of the 1689 Second London Baptist Confession of Faith.
[194] Renihan, *The Mystery of Christ*, 204.

She looks around and notices an American flag waving on top of the U.S. Embassy, and she remembers when she was rescued that she saw that flag on the troops' uniforms. And so, she points up to the flag on the top of the building.

Now, does the young lady mean that the flag itself saved her? That the actual flag rescued her from her oppression? Of course not. She is pointing to what the flag symbolizes. This is how baptism is used in the New Testament. It is a physical symbol of spiritual realities. It is in *this* sense that Peter says baptism saves.

NOT FOR INFANTS

One of the main arguments today between Presbyterians and Baptists is over the mode and subjects of baptism. The argument goes much deeper than water. Phillip Griffiths comments on the baptism debate that being a Baptist should mean more than just "the mode of baptism…Reformed Baptists need to rediscover their rich heritage."[195] Part of that heritage is understanding Baptist covenant theology. Volumes have been written on the subject, so there is not space here to treat it in any sort of fullness.

However, it needs to be said that, historically, Baptists have understood that only believers are included in God's covenant of grace. In the Old Testament, infants were circumcised in the Abrahamic and Mosaic Covenants, ultimately under a covenant of works.[196] This circumcision, though certainly in some senses a gracious sign, did not bring someone into God's covenant of grace. If circumcision was not kept, the children would be cut off from the physical people of God (Gen. 17:14). Circumcision was a work whose ultimate point was to remind physical Israel that they stood in desperate need of One who could fulfill God's Law and then would be cut off for the sake of those who would put their faith in Him (cf. Isa. 53:4-5).

---

[195] Griffiths, *Covenant Theology*, 4.
[196] Reformed Baptists have different views on this. Some see the Abrahamic Covenant as dichotomous in nature. Some early Baptists saw it as two covenants.

The true Israel of both the Old and New Testaments has always and only been *believers* (cf. Rom. 9:6-7). Romans 9:8 says explicitly, "it is not the children of the flesh who are the children of God, but the children of the promise are counted as offspring." Believers are the children of the promise, for only believers are the true children of Abraham. As Paul says in Galatians 3:7, "Know then that it is those of faith who are the sons of Abraham."

As we have discussed in this book, the only way anyone can savingly believe the promises of God is by being born again. So, yes, even members of the covenant of grace in the Old Testament were born again.

Though there are similarities between baptism and circumcision in some ways, Griffiths writes, "Baptism…is both a sign and a seal, marking one as belonging to the spiritual seed of Abraham; sealing the fact that he is united to Christ. The one prerequisite for baptism is that the individual repent and believe. These different criteria hardly suggest parity between these two rites [of circumcision and baptism]."[197] The members of the covenant of grace, then, have always and only been regenerate people, not of a mixed nature. The covenant of grace has never consisted of believers and unbelievers.

The New Covenant, ratified in the blood of Christ, has established water baptism as the outward sign and symbol of an inward reality. Through baptism, when the believer is plunged beneath the surface of the water, he identifies with the death and burial of Christ. When he is lifted out of the water, that is symbolic of Christ's resurrection from the dead and symbolic of the believer himself having new life. By this act, the believer is, in obedience to the Word of God, publicly confessing what has taken place in his heart secretly and sovereignly by the Holy Spirit.

The significance of baptism, then, is clearly only for those who have already been born again. Even James Bannerman, a 19th century paedobaptist, writes, "The immersion in water of the persons of those who are baptized is set forth as their burial with

---

[197] Griffiths, *Covenant Theology*, 68.

Christ in His grave because of sin; and their being raised again out of the water is their resurrection with Christ in His rising again from the dead because of their justification."[198]

Similarly, Louis Berkhof, also a paedobaptist, writing about Christ's Great Commission in Matthew 28:19, says that "They who accepted Christ by faith were to be baptized in the name of the triune God, as a sign and seal of the fact that they had entered into a new relation to God and as such were obliged to live according to the laws of the Kingdom of God."[199]

Bannerman and Berkhof speak properly of baptism in these above quotes. However, they inconsistently apply their understanding of baptism when it comes to infants. Infants have not "entered into a new relation to God" since they are only children of the flesh and have not yet become a son or daughter of Abraham by faith (cf. Galatians 3:7). Nor have they put "off the corruption of nature and ris[en] again into holiness."[200] Thus, the paedobaptist argument is ultimately inconsistent and erroneous.

Though writing centuries *before* Berkhof and Bannerman, 17th Century Baptist, John Spilsbery, pulls no punches in responding to this faulty paedobaptist argumentation, by saying, "[T]o Baptize Infants, makes the holy ordinance of God a lying sign". His argument is that infants cannot participate in all the things the ordinance of Baptism signifies. Things like, "Regeneration and spiritual new birth; a dying and burying with Christ in respect of sin, and a rising with him in a new life to God, and a confirmation of faith in the death and resurrection of Christ, and a free emission of sin by the same". Spilsbery cites 1 Cor.15:29, Rom. 6:3-4, Col. 2:12, 1 Peter 3:21, and Acts 2:38. He says none of these "can be expected in an Infant."[201]

---

[198] James Bannerman, *The Church of Christ: A Treatise on the Nature, Powers, Ordinances, Discipline, and Government of the Christian Church* (Carlisle, PA: Banner of Truth Trust, 2016), 557.

[199] Berkhof, *Systematic Theology*, 624. Berkhof goes on to write, "there is no explicit command in the Bible to baptize children, and that there is not a single instance in which we are plainly told that children were baptized." 632.

[200] Bannerman, *The Church of Christ*, 48.

[201] John Spilsbery, *A Treatise Concerning the Lawfull Subject of Baptism*, Second Edition Corrected and Enlarged (London: Henry Hills, 1652), 41.

That is the point of this entire section. It is not my desire to needlessly take shots at my paedobaptist brothers and sisters. The point is that there is an incontrovertible connection between the ordinance of baptism and regeneration. The latter is inward and performed by the sovereign work of the Holy Spirit. The former is performed by the local church only to those born again as a sign and symbol of what has happened to the new believer.

Do we have to have "regeneration goggles" then in order to know who to Baptize?[202] Of course not. The local church ought to do her best to only baptize believers. Pastors, by examining the confession and life of those wishing to be baptized, must use discernment in making this decision. Sadly, in a fallen world, sometimes local churches can "baptize" unbelievers.

OBEY ACTS 2:38?

My family and I used to live near Stuttgart, AR, which has a beautiful Church of Christ building on one of the main highways in town. On the top of that building it says, "Obey Acts 2:38." What does Acts 2:38 say? "And Peter said to them, 'Repent and be baptized every one of you in the name of Jesus Christ for the forgiveness of your sins, and you will receive the gift of the Holy Spirit.'"

The Church of Christ "denomination" teaches that one does not receive regeneration unless one is baptized. I think it pertinent to our discussion to mention a few notes about Acts 2:38 before moving on from the subject of baptism.

First, some make a grammatical argument from the verse to show that water baptism is not the mechanism for the forgiveness of sins. That is, the text is teaching to be baptized on the basis of forgiveness of sins, not that water baptism is what forgives you. I think grammatical arguments are important and helpful. Really, though, I think it's even simpler than that. I actually think any average Bible reader could understand this if they would just read the Bible in context.

---

[202] "Regeneration Goggles" is a phrase some Paedobaptists have used on social media to insinuate that Baptists need to see the invisible church before being willing to admit someone to the ordinance of baptism.

Curtis Vaughan notes, "To be baptized 'in the name of Jesus Christ,' then, is to acknowledge Him to be all that His name imports. Peter had challenged his audience to accept Jesus as Messiah and Lord. Their baptism in the name of Jesus Christ would be a public acknowledgement that they had done this."[203]

Thus, Acts 2:38 falls in line with all we've been teaching here about baptism. This ordinance is outward evidence of true repentance. Moreover, one only has to read a few more verses to come to Acts 2:41 which says, "So *those who received his word* were baptized, and there were added that day about three thousand souls" (emphasis mine). Then we keep reading on to Acts 3:19, just 25 verses later, and we see Peter preach, "Repent therefore, and turn back, that your sins may be blotted out…"

Baptism, according to Acts, is not the mechanism for regeneration or the forgiveness of sins, but should only be applied to those who receive the Word of God and repent. As we have seen, only those born again do so.

Thus, if the average person will just read the Bible in context, trusting the Holy Spirit, they won't get confused on the matter. If we really want to obey Acts 2:38 in context we will preach to people to repent and believe the gospel, and as a sign of their repentance, they ought to be baptized.

DO I HAVE TO BE BAPTIZED?

From Acts 2:38 we see that for one to refuse to be baptized is a sign that they have actually not repented. Jeff Johnson writes, "Although baptism is not essential to salvation, it is highly unlikely that a person has been truly born again without an eager desire to follow the Lord in this first command that God gives the new Christian (Acts 2:38)."[204]

---

[203] Curtis Vaughan, *Acts*, Founders Study Guide Commentary (Cape Coral, FL: Founders, 2009), 31.
[204] Jeffrey D. Johnson, *The Church: Her Nature, Authority, Purpose, and Worship* (New Albany, MS: Media Gratiae, 2020), 206.

It would have been easy for the Jews to say they believed Peter's message. But Peter showed that true repentance will lead to a person willing to publicly identify with the Lord Jesus Christ in Baptism. Again, Johnson notes, "Baptism is a public confession of Christ (Matt. 10:32-33) that evidences to the church and the world that there has been a radical transformation within."[205]

Baptism is for those who have already received the Holy Spirit through regeneration, and it is not what causes or brings about our regeneration. Rather, baptism is something that a *believer* undergoes. If he is truly born again, he will desire to follow the Lord in believer's baptism because baptism, in the words of Sam Waldron, "says he or she is in union with Christ, is forgiven and has a cleansed heart."[206]

When Jesus talks about being born of the water and the Spirit (John 3:5), He doesn't mean baptism and the Spirit mixed together creates a saving formula. Rather, being "born of the water" is the inward renewal and cleansing we need as prophesied in Ezekiel 36:25-27 and mentioned again in Titus 3:5.

Baptism, then, does not bring about the new birth. A change of heart can only be brought about invisibly and supernaturally by the power of the Holy Spirit alone. Baptism is a physical symbol that shows outwardly what has happened to those born again and closed with faith in Christ having already been united to Him, spiritually cleansed by the Holy Spirit, and justified by grace alone through faith alone.[207] It reminds of that tree where our Savior died, and where we died with Him, and likewise, were brought up to newness of life with Him as well.

The symbolism in baptism matters. This is why we should not sprinkle or pour water over baptismal candidates but instead

---

[205] Johnson, *The Church*, 206.
[206] Waldron, *A Modern Exposition of the 1689 Baptist Confession of Faith*, 407-408.
[207] That's one reason we should be cautious about baptizing young children. I do think it's possible that young children can be genuinely born again. It takes the same grace to save a 4-year-old as it does a 44-year-old. But the biblical issue is the church being sure of what has taken place, and, in our society, I think a lot of people have unfortunately been baptized when they were very young but have since walked away from the faith because they had never actually been born again.

immerse the person fully in water in the name of the Father, Son, and Holy Spirit. Baptism shows how the person has already been spiritually cleansed and is symbolically buried with Christ and raised again to the newness of life.

The point in all of this, of course, is a that the biblical understanding of regeneration also helps us practically with a biblical understanding of the ordinance of Baptism. If we get regeneration right, then it will help us to properly understand the purpose of Baptism and the proper subjects and mode of Baptism.

THE LORD'S SUPPER

Think again about the word visible. Baptism is a visible symbol, and so is the Lord's Supper. God designed the Lord's Supper to show us the symbolic picture of the broken body and shed blood of Christ. And by eating and drinking, it visibly shows us the symbolic picture of trusting the sacrifice of Christ alone for our right standing with God. And by participating in this ordinance together as a local church, it visibly shows us the symbolic picture of believers united together in Christ.

Sam Renihan writes,

> The Lord's Supper has two sides, like Baptism. On the one hand it is God's declaration of the forgiveness of sins to His people in covenant. It is His visible word to them. On the other hand, it is the people's pledge of faith and participation in those promises. We do not simply contemplate the sacraments. We celebrate and enjoy the sacraments. Given that the Lord's Supper, like Baptism, involves active faith in the promises signified by the symbol, it takes on a special character because the church collectively professes its faith in the Lord's Supper...Baptism signifies new creation life. And the Lord's Supper signifies our right to that new creation and ongoing nourishment until we reach it. Even more so, however, the Lord's Supper is the rehearsal dinner

of the great marriage feast of Christ and His bride. Partaking in the one is an anticipation and foretaste of the other. And just as wedding garments are needed for that final feast, they are needed for the initial feast. You cannot make a claim on the present kingdom, the kingdom of grace, without making a claim on the final kingdom, the kingdom of glory.[208]

The Lord's Supper, then, like Baptism, is only for those who have already been born again. It points us to that tree where the body of our Lord was pierced and His blood shed. And in one sense the Lord's Supper is the opposite of Genesis. There God says, "Do not eat." But here at the table, He says, "Come and dine."

This partaking of the Supper is a symbolic act for God's people—those born again. It does not and cannot bring about regeneration. Some denominations are inconsistent regarding these two ordinances because they allow infants to be baptized but forbid their admission to the Lord's Table. The Baptist position is consistent because it says that both ordinances are only for those born again and that all those properly baptized ought to come to the Supper.

The overarching idea is that the Lord's Supper does not bring about our regeneration (or prepare us for justification). Instead, it serves to visually remind us of Christ's sacrifice for His people. As such, only believers are to participate in this significant event.

What then does the Lord's Supper actually do? First, we must emphatically note that the elements in the Lord's Supper, the bread, and the fruit of the vine, remain bread and wine. And we take them in remembrance of Christ.

When Jesus says, "Take, eat, this is my body" (Matt. 26:26), He does not mean this is actually His physical body but it is merely a *symbol* for His body. Just like when Jesus says "I am the door," He does not mean He is an actual, physical door. The fact that Jesus was already physically present with His disciples when He gave this

---

[208] Renihan, *The Mystery of Christ*, 205-206.

command proves that His intention was not for them to think they were both seeing Him and physically eating Him.

When a local church participates in the Lord's Supper, it does so together, remembering Christ. When we do this, He is present with us spiritually, not physically. Through this ordinance, He strengthens our faith and encourages us to press on to the end, through the power of the Holy Spirit.

Also, this ordinance strengthens our unity together as a local church. As local church members partake of the Lord's Supper, they proclaim the Lord's death until He comes (cf. 1 Cor.11:26). This reminds us that the Lord's Supper is to be taken within the context of the local church. It's not an ordinance for weddings or zoom meetings.

It is a dangerous thing to take this ordinance of the Lord's Supper in an unworthy manner (1 Cor.11:27). One way to take this in an unworthy manner is to be unregenerate. An unbeliever has no right to this ordinance because an unbeliever has not been united to Christ by faith. Only those born again are in the saving covenant of Christ and proper subjects of His Table.

It is the Holy Spirit's work to unite us to Christ in this effectual calling, regeneration, and gift of faith. The Lord's Supper is an outward symbol of the inward reality of our union with Christ. Therefore, unregenerate persons remain rebelliously outside of Christ, and all they do when taking the Lord's supper is eat and drink judgment upon themselves.

In this chapter, we have seen that a right understanding of regeneration helps us to properly understand the two ordinances of the local church. To misunderstand regeneration may lead us to misunderstand the two blessed ordinances our Lord Jesus has given to His local churches. We have seen here the biblical affirmation that Baptism and the Lord's Supper do not bring about our new birth. They point us to the tree and are both outward manifestations of what has already occurred in the transformed heart of the believer.

We now move from inside the church to outside. This wonderful doctrine of regeneration ought to be major fuel to believers to participate in biblical evangelism. We will close out the book by examining this truth in our final chapter.

13
BECAUSE AUTHENTIC EVANGELISM IS ESSENTIAL

There is a faulty line of reasoning that says if God is completely sovereign in salvation, choosing whom He will and regenerating whom He will, then evangelism is unnecessary. This argument is an example of fallen men using fallen logic to reject the plain teaching of the Scriptures.

The sovereignty of God in salvation in no way negates the responsibility of believers to proclaim the gospel nor does it lessen the responsibility of sinners to repent of their sins and believe the gospel. As Will Metzger notes, "[W]e should not consider these two doctrines of sovereignty and responsibility as enemies but rather see them the way the Bible does—as friends!"[209]

Those perishing are "perishing, because they refused to love the truth" (2 Thess. 2:10). It is not as though they *wanted* to embrace the truth but were hindered by God. Rather, they *refused* to love the truth.

---

[209] Metzger, *Tell the Truth*, 109.

Calvin rightly notes that they "of their own accord refused salvation."[210]

How then is a person saved? I answered this question early in my first book, *From Death to Life*. "A person is saved when the gospel is proclaimed and the Holy Spirit works through that proclamation in such a way that He moves the sinner from death to life, 'turning on the light'…Only then can a person see his or her sin and turn from it in repentance. Only then can they, by faith, trust in Christ alone as their only suitable and all sufficient Savior."[211]

With this definition in mind, we must remember four key truths:

1. *The gospel must be published indiscriminately*

The gospel is designed to go to every tribe, every tongue, and every nation. Churches must take the gospel to every inch of the globe, proclaiming the good news of salvation in Jesus Christ. This is the external or gospel call whereby all sinners everywhere are to be summoned to come to Christ in repentance and faith.

2. *It is the duty of all men to believe on Christ for salvation*

Unbelief is not merely a "condition" but an act of rebellion. To make a willing decision to refuse to love the truth is inexcusable. It is each person's obligation to savingly look to Christ as their only hope.

3. *There is sufficiency in work of Jesus to cleanse the vilest of sinners*

God invites all sinners, great and small, to partake of Christ. He commands all to repent. He takes no pleasure in the death of the wicked but rather that they turn from their evil ways and live (cf. Ezek. 18:23). No sinner can say, "I don't know if the blood of Christ is enough for me." No sinner can say, "I wonder if God would have me turn from my sin and believe the gospel?"

---

[210] John Calvin and John Pringle, *Commentaries on the Epistles of Paul the Apostle to the Philippians, Colossians, and Thessalonians* (Bellingham, WA: Logos Bible Software, 2010), 338.
[211] Nelson, *From Death to Life*, 5.

4. No one will savingly believe on Christ apart from an efficacious work of divine grace

All men are invited to Christ and commanded to believe. Therefore, we pray for, preach to, and press upon sinners to repent of their sins and close with Christ, i.e., humbly come to Christ, in saving faith. All the while we remember, "The ministry of the word is the pipe or organ; the Spirit of God blowing in it doth effectually change men's hearts...Ministers knock at the door of men's hearts, the Spirit comes with a key and opens the door."[212]

WHAT IS EVANGELISM?

We get the English word "evangelism" from the Greek word εὐαγγελίζω *(euaggelizo)*. This word is used in Luke 2:10, where the angel tells the shepherds, "Fear not, for behold, I bring you good news of great joy that will be for all the people." The verb, εὐαγγελίζω, is to "bring good news."

A basic definition of evangelism, then, is simply announcing, proclaiming, teaching, preaching, or sharing the good news of the life, death, burial, and resurrection of Jesus for our sins to lost persons. This is done with words – either spoken, preached, or written.

Paul uses the same word from Luke 2:10 in Ephesians 3:8 when he writes, "To me, though I am the very least of all the saints, this grace was given, 'εὐαγγελίζω[213] the Gentiles." The ESV and NASB translate this word as "to preach to." The CSB says "to proclaim to." This is because Biblical evangelism is communicating in audible (or written) words, "that Christ died for our sins in accordance with the Scriptures, that he was buried, that he was raised on the third day in accordance with the Scriptures" (1 Cor. 15:3-4).[214]

---

[212] Thomas Watson, *The Select Works of the Rev. Thomas Watson, Comprising His Celebrated Body of Divinity, in a Series of Lectures on the Shorter Catechism, and Various Sermons and Treatises* (New York: Robert Carter & Brothers, 1855), 148.

[213] εὐαγγελίσασθα

[214] I would also add, "We haven't finished proclaiming the gospel until we include what is demanded of the people hearing it—repentance from sin and faith in Christ." Nelson, *From Death to Life*, 38.

For this chapter, I want to keep this expansive definition of evangelism. By evangelism, I am referring to how we talk to our children about salvation. I mean how we talk to our neighbors about the gospel. I am including how some might dialogue with lost persons after a sermon. I am advocating preaching in the streets and going door to door. By evangelism, I am simply concerned with how Christians talk to lost people about their need for Christ and how one becomes a Christian.

So, here is the question I have for us: How are we to "close the deal," so to speak? How do we get someone over that line from being a non-Christian to a Christian? What is it that we need to do to get a lost person born again? How does this *work?*

Well, here is why a right understanding of the doctrine of regeneration is essential. If you don't understand how grilling works, how will you ever cook a good steak? If you don't know how evangelism "works," how can we expect to see sinners genuinely converted?

If we hope to see people savingly embrace the glorious message of the gospel of Jesus Christ, we need to both know the truth of how God works in salvation and proclaim this truth in its fullness to those who need to hear it – every sinner on the planet.

Do you remember when we discussed the end of John 2? Sadly, I believe most in today's evangelicalism would have stopped at v.23, where many "believed." They would have baptized them. They would have signed them up to serve on a ministry team, teach Sunday school, or be a deacon or pastor. And yet, the people in John 2:23 were not born again. So, how does this work?

THE COMMON WAY

The first thing I want to address is how "closing the deal" is *commonly* done, at least in the experience of many conservative evangelicals today. Someone wants to become a Christian, and what is the reaction?

Well, first, maybe the Christian asks the lost person a few questions. Do you understand sin? Do you know the gospel?

Do you want to live for Jesus? Stuff like that. And then, if those questions are answered adequately, a prayer is recited, with the intent that it be sincere. It is in that moment, it is claimed, that if a person really meant it, he or she becomes a Christian.

We have all probably seen this done. Or, if you are like me, you've actually had other people pray the so-called "sinner's prayer" because this is how you were taught to lead someone to Christ.

So, an event takes place, maybe a church camp or evangelistic meeting, where people come up to the front at the end of a service and maybe there are several people – I see that hand! – and they are asked to recite a prayer that the preacher says. They all "believe" in Jesus! And then in some cases these "believers" are declared Christians there on the spot and sometimes even told to write the date down in their Bibles and never to doubt what happened to them.

I have more than a few problems with that methodology. And you should too. The first problem is that this approach is found nowhere in the Scriptures. The Biblical invitation is much different. It is to believe on Jesus as *Lord*. An old Southern Baptist evangelist, Rolfe Barnard (1904-1969), said it this way, "Those who pervert the Gospel beg people to accept Jesus as their Saviour, and they will be saved. That is a lie out of Hell, because it is not in the Bible. If a person does not surrender to Jesus Christ as your Lord to rule and reign over you — Why! — You are not saved!"[215]

Another problem I have with the "sinner's prayer" type methodology is not only is this approach not in the Bible, but it also stands in blatant contradiction to things that we *do have* in the Bible. For example, we've looked several times at John 6:63, which says, "It is the Spirit who gives life; the flesh is no help at all." Or John 1:12-13 which says, "But to all who did receive him, who believed in his name, he gave the right to become children of God, *who were born, not of blood nor of the will of the flesh nor of the will of man*, but of God."

---

[215] Accessed: https://faithbaptistwauseon.com/Difference%20Between%20the%20Old%20and%20New%20Gospel.html

Sinners receive Christ because of God's initiating and effectual work. It's not something we meet God halfway on. It's not the will of the flesh that brings about the new birth but the will of God. As Joel Beeke notes, "both preacher and listener are totally dependent on the work of the Spirit to effect regeneration and conversion when, how, and in whom He will."[216]

The third reason I have a problem with the altar call and "sinner's prayer" methodology is that it's absent from church history for the first 18 centuries. Now, if it were in the Bible, that would be enough. But the fact that it's not in the Bible, and that it runs counter to things we see in the Bible, and that for 1800 years it could not be found in churches anywhere, should send red flags up everywhere for us.

FINNEY-ISM REVIVED

Cue the ominous music. We are back to Charles Grandison Finney (1792-1875). As a recap, Finney made his debut during The Second Great Awakening (the high point being the early 1830s) in America. Finney was instrumental in what was known as "the new measures" where people would come up to the front of the meeting space during or at the end of a service if they wanted to "get saved." Prior to these "new measures," this is not how evangelism worked.

These questionable methods bled over into people like Billy Sunday (1862-1935) and Dwight Moody (1837-1899). More famously, Billy Graham (1918-2018) applied these methods in his "Just As I Am" altar calls which resulted in thousands of people coming forward to profess allegiance to Christ.

I am grateful for many things about Billy Graham, but he was wrong on this. He said things like,

> I'm going to ask you to come forward. Up there—down there—I want you to come. You come right now—

---

[216] Joel R. Beeke, *Puritan Evangelism: A Biblical Approach*, 2nd Edition (Grand Rapids: Reformation Heritage, 2007), 72.

quickly. If you are here with friends or relatives, they will wait for you. Don't let distance keep you from Christ. It's a long way, but Christ went all the way to the cross because He loved you. Certainly you can come these few steps and give your life to Him...[217]

Graham is saying that the physical act of moving from one location to another will answer your spiritual problem with Christ. This methodology has led to a high number of false converts. Studies have shown that sometimes as low as 2-4% of people who come forward at events like that are still in church five years later.[218] And there is no allegiance to Christ without fidelity to His bride.

To put this in perspective, let's say you have an event or evangelistic service or crusade or church camp and 100 people come forward. You post to social media that 100 people became Christians and you're thrilled. But if those 100 people were studied for five years, it is possible that only two to four of them were still in church and devoted to Christ. Out of 100 people, those were the only genuinely born again believers.

Why is this? This is because, ultimately, our theology drives our methodology. What we believe manifests itself in what we do. You can tell me what you believe all day long, but I know what you believe by how you live.

Most people I know personally will bend over backward to say things like, "This prayer won't save you. Coming forward won't save you. It's all God." I am certainly appreciative of those sorts of qualifications. However, what are we really communicating when we continue to use this faulty methodology? "You take the first step, and God will do the rest!"

Why would we continue to use this methodology if it's not in the Bible, actually runs contrary to the Bible, and if it was not

---

[217] Jim Ehrhard, "The Dangers of the Invitation System," Reformation and Revival 2, no. 3 (1993), 80.
[218] https://www.ccwtoday.org/2009/04/ the-corrupt-root-and-bitter-fruit-of-altar-call-evangelism/

found in Christianity for over 1800 years? The answer is that it is so woven into our evangelical tradition by now that we do not know another way.

This is why understanding regeneration matters. When we rightly understand the doctrine of regeneration, we will replace these faulty methods with a biblical practice. We will repudiate Finney-ism and seek a more biblical approach to evangelizing lost souls.

THE BIBLICAL WAY

If we believe in this biblical doctrine of regeneration and trust the power of God, what do we do to see sinners savingly converted to Christ? Am I saying we just do nothing? Of course not! W.B. Sprague rightly lectured, "[If] the doctrine of divine influence be preached in such a way as to authorize the inference that man has nothing to do in respect to his salvation, but wait to be operated upon like a mere machine…there is little probability that [people] will be converted."[219]

What did we see Paul tell the Philippian jailer? Believe! (Acts 16:31). He did not say, "Wait to see if you are elect." Or "Wait to see if you will be regenerated!" Instead, he gave him the imperative, *Believe*. It was the jailer's *duty* to believe on Christ.

Revelation 22:17 declares, "The Spirit and the Bride say, 'Come.' And let the one who hears say, 'Come.' And let the one who is thirsty come; let the one who desires take the water of life without price." All men, women, boys, and girls are invited (and commanded) to come to Christ in saving faith.

We are to declare this proclamation to the uttermost parts of the earth. Trust, dear soul. Come to Christ! Repent of your sins and believe the gospel! This goes to all sinners regardless of our assessment of their situation. All we need to know is they are sinners. We have been commanded to share the gospel with them, and God is willing to use the proclamation of His gospel to save many.

---

[219] William B. Sprague, *Lectures on Revivals of Religion* (London: Banner of Truth Trust, 1959), 84.

Both in Scripture and history we see the circumstances surrounding conversion happen in a variety of ways. Charles Spurgeon heard a sermon from a layperson in the midst of a wintry storm. George Whitefield read a book by Henry Scougal. John Newton recalled Scripture he had memorized as a child. The Philippian jailer was on the brink of committing suicide.

But all of these stories, in fact all conversion stories, are tied to the gospel's proclamation and a conscious and intentional response of faith. That response of faith is a reaction to the Spirit's effectual calling and sovereign gifting. We don't have control over that. It is not our business to control the wind but to preach the Word. It is our duty to "implore [sinners] on behalf of Christ, be reconciled to God" (2 Cor.5:20).

THE EXTERNAL CALL

If we really believe the Bible's teaching on regeneration, if we really believe that being born again is totally a work of God, then what *do* we do?

First, we proclaim the gospel. Paul says in Romans 10:17, "So faith comes from hearing, and hearing through the word of Christ." We must get the gospel right. As John Domm notes, "It is not reasonable to expect the Spirit of truth to empower a false, defective gospel."[220] Thus, we proclaim the right gospel, rightly. And in doing so, we issue the external call mentioned at the beginning of this chapter.

It all begins with the gospel. Will Metzger writes, "[A] big difference between biblical evangelism and modern evangelism [is] a whole gospel versus a truncated gospel; a message-centered gospel versus a method-centered gospel; [and] a God-centered gospel versus a me-gospel."[221] We proclaim the whole, message-centered, God-centered gospel to the whole person. Whether they are young or old, tall or short, boy or girl, or any shade of skin color, they need the robust, biblical, God-glorifying gospel of Jesus Christ.

---

[220] Ventura, *A New Exposition of the London Baptist Confession of Faith of 1689*, 161.
[221] Metzger, *Tell the Truth*, 38-39.

The gospel, in sum, is that Christ was crucified for our sins to appease the righteous wrath of God that stood against us and rose again for our justification. A person cannot understand the gospel apart from understanding sin and how we have broken God's Law and deserve His judgment. Apart from Christ, all persons are sinners in need of redemption and deserving of hell, not folks who've just made a mistake here or there but would be a really awesome addition to God's team. God loves you, or try Jesus and see what happens – those things are not the gospel.

Sinners are not just in a "messy" situation. They are in a *perilous* position. The judgment of our holy and sovereign God hangs over their heads. They are children of wrath. Their only hope for a right standing with God is the finished work of Jesus Christ. What sinners need, then, is the sin atoning, soul-restoring, the self-abasing gospel of Jesus Christ.

In counseling a lost sinner, W.B. Sprague said we must "teach him what God has done for his salvation; and what God requires him to do; and the reasonableness of that requirement; and the necessity of it being complied with."[222] Teach the lost man the gospel. Teach him what God requires him to do: Repent – which may mean we need to explain that word more depending on the context – and also believe, which we may need to explain more as well.[223]

Teach him the reasonableness of that requirement – meaning, God is right and good and holy, and it is not unreasonable for a person to repent and believe the gospel. In fact, it is the height of unreasonableness for a person not to repent of his or her sins and believe the good news of Jesus Christ.

Next, the convicted sinner should be counseled to help him understand repentance and faith and to use the means of grace, such as Bible reading or time with God in prayer, while understanding that these means of grace are not substitutes for repentance and faith.[224] The point is, the sinner is not supposed to sit around and

---

[222] Sprague, *Lectures on Revivals*, 157.
[223] I define repentance and faith more fully in chapter 5 of *From Death to Life*.
[224] Sprague, *Lectures on Revivals*, Chapter 6.

see if God will regenerate Him. It is his duty to call upon Christ and turn form his sins.

The sinner should also know that there are wrong ways to come to Jesus, like the way of self-righteousness (as if Jesus owes you), or only seeking comfort from a guilty conscience rather than obedience to Christ's beckoning. Or today, there is the ever-popular "Come to Christ so you can get [fill in the blank]." And whatever one puts in that blank is idolatry. We come to Christ to get Christ. He is the treasure of the gospel.

There are no shortcuts on the road to genuine conversions. Again, it is not that conversions to Christ cannot happen quickly. They certainly can, and the moment of regeneration and conversion is instantaneous. God does not bring about regeneration in various stages but in one sweeping moment of love, mercy, and grace to the undeserving sinner.

The time counseling a lost person, though, might be several meetings or weeks or perhaps months on occasion, and this requires godly wisdom, genuine compassion, humble patience, and love for the truth. There is no quick "pray this prayer" that magically moves a sinner from death to life. The most important thing is their exposure to the gospel (cf. Rom. 1:16).

Finally, let me remind us that we don't merely give sinners the gospel; we also call them to come to Christ in faith. No, we can't reach inside their hearts. But our voices can reach their ears, and we call them to rest in Jesus – that if they come to Him in faith, He will save their souls.

Thus, the sinner should be exhorted to close with Christ immediately (in the Puritan vernacular) and warned that to delay is to only increase guilt. It is biblical to implore the person to come to Christ. *Implore* is the word we saw above in 2 Corinthians 5:20, where Paul is "summing up the appeal he gives to all the world." The Greek word, δέομαι, means "to ask for with urgency, with the implication of presumed need—'to plead, to beg.'"[225] We plead with sinners to come to Christ.

---

[225] Johannes P. Louw and Eugene Albert Nida, *Greek-English Lexicon of the New Testament: Based on Semantic Domains* (New York: United Bible Societies, 1996), 407.

"CLOSING THE DEAL"

Okay, so what if a person seems to understand the gospel, sin, and repentance, and can check off all the boxes so to speak? Then what do we do? How do we "close the deal?" This can be difficult because of our genuine desire to see sinners saved. We desperately want to see our children saved. We desire to see our neighbors converted to Christ. We want to see that lost family visiting our church to be born again.

So, what do we do? We tell them to call out to Christ. Tell them to believe on the Lord Jesus. Tell them to repent of their sins and close with Christ in faith.

God will not believe for a person. Johnson notes, "God…does not force the elect to repent and believe in Christ against their wills."[226] He or she, therefore, must willingly turn from sin and believe on Christ in order to be saved. As Murray writes, "It is not God who believes in Christ for salvation, it is the sinner. It is by God's grace that a person is able to believe, but faith is an activity on the part of the person."[227]

Perhaps those searching for salvation need to go home to spend time with the Lord in prayer or read specific passages of Scripture. Perhaps they'll desire to accept the Lord on the spot. If they do, let me urge you to allow them to pray from their own hearts

What if they don't know how to pray? You explain to them that they are merely to talk to God. Perhaps this is a place you are able to ascertain if they truly understand the gospel or not.

Are they saying something along the lines of "God, be merciful to me, a sinner?" Or, are they praying for their grandmother or new job or worldly riches? If it's the latter, they probably do not yet understand the gospel, and if you supply the words they are just supposed to say, then you haven't helped the situation. In fact, you've only worsened it.

---

[226] Johnson, *The Sovereignty of God*, 156.
[227] Murray, *Redemption Accomplished and Applied*, 111.

We must believe Jeremiah 17:9. As Calvin wrote, "The human heart has so many recesses for vanity, so many lurking places for falsehood, is so shrouded by fraud and hypocrisy, that it often deceives itself."[228]

People can try to close with Christ for the wrong reasons. They can try to close with Christ for self-righteous motivations. They can try to merely assuage a guilty conscience. They can see other people doing it and feel peer pressure. They can just not want to go to hell.

What lost persons need is *a change of heart*. God alone does this, and God does this alone. Why was the result of Paul's preaching that "some were convinced by what he said, but others disbelieved" (Acts 28:24)? The sovereign grace of God is the answer. The external call is indiscriminate, but God's sovereign efficacious grace is discriminate. He saves whom He will for His own glory (see Acts 13:48).

We proclaim the treasure of Christ. We extol His glories. We do all we can to show sinners the surpassing value and worth of knowing King Jesus. But at the end of the day, only God can remove the veil over the lost person's heart so that he or she sees the inestimable riches of Christ and bows the knee to Him in repentance and faith.

We must be willing to labor with sinners, in several meetings if necessary, trusting that God works through the gospel to open blinded eyes. We must also trust that God works through His means of grace. That is, tell the sinner to wrestle with God in prayer. Tell the sinner to read the Scriptures since they "reviv[e] the soul" (Ps. 19:7).[229]

No, these means do not take the place of faith and repentance. But they are channels the Holy Spirit is pleased to work through as He will according to His own sovereign pleasure and in accordance with the eternal counsels of the triune God.

We must, therefore, depend upon the Spirit to work as He will. This brings us tremendous hope and great relief. I don't have to be a

---

[228] Calvin, *Institutes of the Christian Religion*, Vol. 2, 107.
[229] As Calvin writes, "it is always by his word that [God] manifests himself to those whom he designs to draw to himself." *Institutes of the Christian Religion*, Vol. 2, 102.

"salesman." I don't have to use underhanded ways or cheap stunts. I don't have to offer door prizes. God is going to save through the heralding of His gospel. When I take the gospel to my children, or neighbors, or the ends of the earth, I know that God is going to save through it.

I do not have to peel back the curtain to peer into God's eternal decrees in order to ascertain whether or not I should preach the gospel to this or that person. I am free, by God's Word, to proclaim to any and all sinners the good news of the gospel as I trust God to work as He will. Actually, I am more than merely "free" to share the gospel to all; I am duty-bound by the inerrant, infallible, authoritative, sufficient Scriptures to share the gospel with all! And I really can trust the sovereign Lord of heaven with the salvation of sinners.

Sure, I may have to labor years like Adoniram Judson. Or I may not ever see the full fruit of my labor this side of heaven. But I can confidently scatter the seed of the gospel knowing that God has promised to use it. Satan will block some seed. Some will be scattered on resisting or worldly hearts. But some will find good soil because God Himself is working in the hearts of men to receive it.

Not every evangelistic encounter will end in someone being born again. Many, in fact, won't. But we can still confidently share the gospel, whether it's preaching on the street, having a conversation over coffee, or passing out tracts, knowing that, somewhere down the road, perhaps someone else may build on the foundation we have laid. Truly, we won't know till heaven the impact that sharing the gospel has had here on earth. So, share away, with confidence in the God who saves sinners for His own eternal glory.

THE FREE OFFER OF THE GOSPEL

We must maintain that regeneration is an instantaneous act of God in people's hearts through gospel proclamation. "Of his own will he brought us forth by the word of truth," (James 1:18). Ultimately, what I am saying is Jonah 2:9: "Salvation belongs to Yahweh."

BECAUSE AUTHENTIC EVANGELISM IS ESSENTIAL

At the end of the day, we don't close the deal with anyone. We do not bring any unregenerate soul across the finish line. We don't bring any sinner from death to life. This is all God's doing. At the same time, Christians and churches are duty-bound to carry the gospel message to all lands, peoples, and nations and proclaim the free offer of the gospel.

Why are we not more evangelistic? Those who rightly hold to monergistic regeneration must be today's greatest evangelists! Don't tell me you're a Calvinist if you don't care about the souls of others. Don't tell me you care about sound theology if you don't care about the glory Christ receives as He is proclaimed to sinners. Those serious about regeneration are serious about evangelism.

This ought to manifest itself in preaching the gospel at public venues when possible. It ought to be you handing out a tract to those around you at the gas pumps. It should be you engaging your waitress in conversation, when possible, to inquire as to the state of her soul. It for sure ought to mean that there is not a house within reasonable distance from your church that has not been visited in some way by members of your local body for the express purpose of telling them the good news of King Jesus and how He requires them to repent of their sins and believe His gospel and how "God will not turn anyone away who sincerely comes to Christ in faith."[230]

John Murray wrote, "God entreats, he invites, he commands, he calls, he presents the overture of mercy and grace, and he does this to all without distinction or discrimination."[231] Thus, the offer of the gospel is meant to be heralded freely and indiscriminately to all persons. Let's get busy!

Similarly, John Owen said, "*Preachers of the gospel* and others have sufficient warrant to press upon all men the duties of faith, repentance, and obedience, although they know that in themselves they have not a sufficiency of ability for their due performance." He goes on to argue that this is because we are "not to consider what man can do or will do, but what God requires."[232]

---

[230] Johnson, *The Sovereignty of God*, 157.
[231] Murray, *Redemption Accomplished and Applied*, 112.
[232] Owen, *The Works of John Owen*, Vol. 3, 295.

In other words, we don't have the right to decide what a man can or cannot do. Christ commands His followers to proclaim the gospel and call all sinners everywhere to repentance and faith in Him.

Owen also rightly points out that gospel proclamation to unregenerate persons, including calling them to come to Christ, is "[t]o exercise a means appointed of God for their *conversion*, or the communication of saving grace unto them." God uses our commanding sinners to repent and believe the gospel "to communicate of his grace unto the souls of men; not with respect unto them as their duties, but as they are ways appointed and sanctified by him unto such ends."[233]

Thus, every Christian must share the gospel with unregenerate sinners regardless of their unwillingness and inability. Through this endeavor, God actually communicates saving grace to those whom He will (cf. Rom. 9:16, 1 Peter 1:3). Therefore, we must be willing to share the gospel, not holding back any of its glorious truths. We must share the gospel and press on all men, women, boys, and girls the duties of repentance, faith, and obedience. Woe to us if we don't!

We counsel. We explain. We exhort. We plead. We pray. We point people to Jesus as their only suitable and all-sufficient Savior. We can even rightly say with full integrity that "God desires that all people be saved, a desire which is manifested in His indiscriminate offer of the gospel to all people."[234] The very fact that a lost person is hearing the gospel message is a testimony to God's grace and His genuine willingness to make good on His promises to any person who believes on Christ.

But at the end of the day, regeneration is monergistic. It's not the sinner's work. It is God's sovereign work alone.

THEOLOGY MATTERS

Theology matters. Theology produces methodology. The doctrine of regeneration is practical because it shows us how to properly

---
[233] Owen, *The Works of John Owen*, Vol. 3, 295.
[234] Barrett and Nettles, *Whomever He Wills*, 124. See Ezek. 18:23, 18:32, 33:11.

understand evangelism. It is not my job to bring sinners from death to life. My job is to faithfully proclaim God's message of mercy to the world and trust Him with the harvest.

I understand that what I am saying can be frustrating because we want to see immediate bona fide results, don't we? And this will move us away from our microwave-evangelism society a bit and cause us to be more careful in articulating the gospel and its required response and even the important work of evaluating fruit rather than just running people through an assembly line.

We must keep these truths in mind. The gospel is to go out to all people. It is the duty of all men to believe on Christ for salvation. There is sufficiency in the death, burial, and resurrection of Jesus to cleanse the vilest of sinners. No one will savingly believe on Christ apart from an efficacious work of divine grace.

There are no shortcuts. Regeneration is a sovereign work of God. This changes our evangelistic methodology away from gimmickry and toward faithfulness to the Scriptures because we are after God's glory. And we are filled with hope knowing that Jesus *will* save His people from their sins (cf. Matt. 1:21). Therefore, we preach, pray, and plead, and we trust God to do His work.

NO GIMMICKS

In Matthew 16:18 Jesus says, "I will build my church, and the gates of hell shall not prevail against it." Gates are not an offensive weapon. Hell is on the defensive and the church of Christ is on the offensive.

Homer tells the story of the Trojan War. The city of Troy was so impenetrable that the Greek armies could not breach it for ten years. Then one day they had an idea. They would build a large wooden horse and put men inside of it to open the gates. They would pretend to leave, and the Trojans would bring the horse inside thinking it was a gift. According to Homer, this subterfuge worked!

When it comes to the church's mission, however, no deception is needed. Though the "gates of hell" are ten thousand times stronger than the gates of Troy, the church doesn't have to sneak in to rescue sinners. We announce with boldness, "We are coming through, and you cannot stop us!"

We do not have to come up with phony ploys in order to get people in the kingdom. We barge through with the gospel of our Lord Jesus Christ with complete and desperate dependence upon the Holy Spirit and we see sinners saved according to the eternal decree of our sovereign God for the glory of His holy name. Be encouraged with this truth and go and share the gospel!

CONCLUSION

Understanding regeneration biblically matters practically. It helps us to submit to the teaching of the Scriptures properly. It strengthens our view of the Holy Spirit. It brings glory to God in our salvation. It gives us the proper perspective of man. It aids us in proper evangelistic methodology. It helps to give us a proper view of the ordinances. And it even helps us understand who makes up the local church.

So many other chapters could have been written. For example, we could have spent a whole chapter on sanctification and its connection to regeneration. Believers walk in holiness because God has caused them to be born again. This is the connection Peter makes in 1 Peter 1:3-16.

We have focused instead upon the Bible, the Holy Spirit, God's glory, evangelism, the ordinances, and the local church. These realities have been given in an effort to encourage you to see the practicality of sound doctrine.

In closing this work, I'd like to issue a gospel appeal in the unlikely event that an unbeliever may have read to the end of this book. I implore you to come to Christ right now in faith. Turn to Him as the Lord as Savior of your life.

As Romans 10:9-10 says, "If you confess with your mouth that Jesus is Lord and believe in your heart that God raised him from the dead, you will be saved. For with the heart one believes and is justified, and with the mouth one confesses and is saved."

BECAUSE AUTHENTIC EVANGELISM IS ESSENTIAL

In the words of Richard Sibbes, I say, "[T]hough we be all dead, even the best of us, by nature, yet let us use the parts of nature that we have, that God hath given us, to offer ourselves to the gracious and blessed means wherein the Spirit of God may work."[235]

Yes, you are spiritually dead, but that hasn't kept you from reading this book! Will you then consider what you've read? Turn to the Scriptures – read John 3:16, for example – and go to the Lord in prayer, asking Him to help your unbelief.[236]

John Bunyan preached,

> O grace! O amazing grace! To see a prince entreat a beggar to receive an alms would be a strange sight; to see a king entreat the traitor to accept of mercy would be a stranger sight than that; but to see God entreat a sinner, to hear Christ say, "I stand at the door and knock," with a heart full and a heaven full of grace to bestow upon him that opens, this is such a sight as dazzles the eyes of angels.[237]

What a grace that the King of kings would in no wise cast you out if you came to him right now in faith (cf. John 6:37, KJV)! Do not use unbelief as an excuse. It's not an excuse. It is a sin.

Look to Christ now in faith. He is altogether lovely. Oh, that your heart would treasure Him!

---

[235] Richard Sibbes, *The Complete Works of Richard Sibbes*, ed. Alexander Balloch Grosart, Vol. 4 (Edinburgh; London; Dublin: James Nichol; James Nisbet and Co.; W. Robertson, 1863), Vol. 7, 404.

[236] Reformed theologian William Shedd, wrote, "To the person who inquires: 'How am I to obtain the new birth, and what particular thing am I to do respecting it' the answer is: 'Find out that you need it and that your self-enslaved will cannot originate it. And when you have found this out, cry unto God the Holy Spirit, 'Create in me a clean heart, and renew within me a right spirit.'" And this prayer must not cease until the answer comes, as Christ teaches in the parable of the widow and the unjust judge (Luke 18:1–8).William Greenough Thayer Shedd, *Dogmatic Theology*, ed. Alan W. Gomes, 3rd ed. (Phillipsburg, NJ: P&R, 2003), 775.

[237] Bunyan, *Saved by Grace*, Vol. 1, 350.

Repent of your sins and believe His gospel! Cling to Christ. Call out to the Lord who is abundant in mercy. Forsake your sins and your unbelief. He is ready to receive the vilest of offenders. It is not your job to control the wind. It blows where it will. It is your job to believe on Christ. Do so even now.

If you do, it is because you have had a change of heart. To God alone be the glory.

Appendix:
JOHN FLAVEL ON THE GLORY OF GOD'S WORK IN REGENERATION

Let every new creature be cheerful and thankful: if God hath renewed your natures, and thus altered the frame and temper of your hearts, he hath bestowed the richest mercy upon you that heaven or earth affords. This is a work of the greatest rarity; a new creature, may be called, One among a thousand: it is also an everlasting work, never to be destroyed, as all other natural works of God (how excellent soever) must be: it is a work carried on by Almighty Power, through unspeakable difficulties and mighty oppositions, Eph. 1:12.

The exceeding greatness of God's power goes forth to produce it; and indeed no less is required to enlighten the blind mind, break the rocky heart, and bow the stubborn will of man; and the same Almighty Power which at first created it, is necessary to be continued every moment to preserve and continue it, 1 Pet. 1:5.

The new creature is a mercy which draws a train of innumerable and invaluable mercies after it, Eph. 2:13, 14. 1 Cor. 3:20. When God hath given us a new nature, then he dignifies us with a *new name*, Rev. 2:17. brings us into a *new covenant*, Jer. 31:33. begets us again to a *new hope*, 1 Pet. 1:3. Intitles [sic] us to a *new inheritance*, John 1:12, 13.

It is the new creature which through Christ makes our persons and duties acceptable with God, Gal. 6:15. In a word, it is the wonderful work of God, of which we may say, "This is the Lord's doing, and it is marvellous in our eyes." There are unsearchable wonders in its *generation,* in its *operation,* and in its *preservation.* Let all therefore, whom the Lord hath thus renewed, fall down at the feet of God, in an humble admiration of the unsearchable riches of free grace, and never open their mouths to complain under any adverse or bitter providences of God.[238]

---

[238] Flavel, *The Whole Works of the Reverend John Flavel,* Vol. 2, 367.

On Campus & Distance Options Available

GRACE BIBLE THEOLOGICAL SEMINARY

Interested in becoming a student or supporting our ministry?
Please visit gbtseminary.org

Other Books by Free Grace Press

The Living Epistle
  by Cornelius Tyree

The Sovereignty of God
  by Jeffrey D. Johnson

God the Preacher and Apologist
  by Lance Quinn

The Exorcism of Satan
  by Joshua P. Howard

Love and Its Fruits: Jonathan Edwards' Charity and Its Fruits, Summarized for the 21st Century
  by Daniel Chamberlin

A Portrait of God: Stephen Charnock's Discourses upon the Existence and Attributes of God, Summarized for the 21st Century
  by Daniel Chamberlin

A Commentary on Galatians
  by Tom Nettles and Sylvia Nettles Dickson

Basic Christian Doctrines
  by Curt Daniel

The Gospel Made Clear to Children
  by Jennifer Adams

Ten Essential Sermons of Charles Spurgeon
  by Charles Spurgeon

Saving Natural Theology from Thomas Aquinas
  by Jeffrey D. Johnson